recollections

and recipes

Bill Buffett

To Joe
Bill Buffett
May, 2014

Contents

preface

Fifteen years ago I got the urge to write a book about my life. I made lists of dates and events. I still find these early efforts in old files. Years passed. I assembled a book on my mother, *Dear Katherine,* and one on my family's grocery store in Omaha, Nebraska, *Foods You Will Enjoy.*

But I put off writing about myself. I had to work through thoughts like who would be interested, and why I should bother. Two revelations helped me. First, I realized I wasn't writing for everyone. I wanted my audience to be family and friends. That took some pressure off. Second, I figured out I didn't have to write an autobiography. To begin at my beginning and continue to the present seemed both daunting and dull.

I decided to write about specific memories and events. My family's enthusiasm for the project also heartened me, as did the encouragement and friendship of both Carol Henderson, my editor, and Rick Rawlins, who designed the book.

Thirty-four essays and twenty family recipes comprise this collection. I hope you enjoy it and also hope that you will pick up a pen or sit down at a computer and write your own stories—for those who are coming along.

great plains

viaduct

roosevelt   white leghorns   city slicker

britches

chokecherry jam

fly swatter

sorghum field   barbed wire

prairie dogs   republican river

burlington

dog-eared

flickering zephyr

black satchel   train #32

NO PLACE LIKE

NEBRASKA

hired men

ripley's
miss rasmussen
heavy muslin
foot treadle
buried cistern
screen door
hand pump
ivory soap
rich soil
headless bird
pinfeathers
chalk cliffs
herd of buffalo
bag of popcorn
butterscotch sundaes
c and h sugar
beals elementary
heavy barbell
air force
mother, may i
white bungalow
bohemian meat market
wimpy streak
patched housecoat
mahogany box
catholic school
ak-sar-ben
face tag
omaha knights
textbook tourniquet
spin-the-bottle

Hasty in Hastings

To get to my grandmother's farm when I was a young boy, I'd take the train from Omaha and get off in Hastings. After a long wait, I'd board a bus to Red Cloud.

One summer I got off the train and headed to the station more rapidly than usual. I found the men's room and pushed open the door. I spotted several potted palms on the floor but no urinals. Unusual as it was, I did see four wooden doors behind which I knew I'd find toilets. I pushed one open and there sat a woman. I still remember her every word: "I'm afraid you're in the wrong place, sonny."

I hastened out, took a quick left, and entered the station's luncheonette. Near the stools stood a comic book rack. I hid behind it until I saw the woman, finished and reassembled, leave the station. I was sure the door had said "MEN." What happened? Returning to the site of my embarrassment, I understood. Yes, the letters M-E-N appeared, but a W and an O preceded them. The door was inset and, coming down the hall, I'd looked up at just that moment when the frame blocked the W and the O.

Even today, I try to be thankful that the woman and I were not on the same bus to Red Cloud. After seventy years my chagrin lingers.

grammy's potato rolls

1 package **yeast**, ¾ cup warm **water**, 1 cup mashed **potatoes**, 1½ cups **milk**, 7½ cups **flour**, ⅔ cup **butter**, ⅔ cup **sugar**, 1½ teaspoons **salt**, 2 **eggs**

Dissolve the yeast in warm water. Add the mashed potatoes, milk, and about a cup of the flour to make a smooth batter. Set in a warm place overnight.

Cream the butter, sugar, and salt. Add with well-beaten eggs to the yeast-potato mixture. Add the remaining flour and mix well. Knead the dough gently until it is smooth then let it rise in a greased bowl until double.

Flour your hands. Punch the dough down and shape it into balls about half the size of tennis balls. Place in greased pans. Let rise to double and bake at 425 for 15 minutes. If tops brown too fast, cover loosely with foil.

Night Train Through Inavale

Growing up on the Great Plains in the 1940s, I often traveled by train. I loved everything about them. Sometimes my parents would take my brother and me to a viaduct in the country just beyond the Omaha city limits. Surrounded by cornfields, we would look to the west and soon would see a wisp of smoke against the red-hued sky of the Nebraska prairie. The wisp grew as it rose from the iron horse beneath it. Coming fast—with a roar, a whoosh of black smoke, and cars behind it—the locomotive thundered under the viaduct. We'd dash to the other side and watch it hurtle toward the city.

I spent hours watching these awesome machines. Coal smoke gave them a distinctive smell, and into my ears came the clang of the engine's bell, the piercing whistle, the escape of steam, and the click-clack of cars over tracks. Trains were a presence that nothing has replaced. When a train pulled in, nobody was looking the other way.

The train I remember best was the Burlington Route's night train through Inavale. For me, that train carries memories of summers spent with my grandmother at her farm near Red Cloud. My memories are as present and bright as stars in Nebraska's night sky. It was to this hallowed ground that I came every summer from the age of three to the age of fifteen.

Mildred Norris, later our "Grammy," had come west from Pennsylvania in 1877 with her parents and eleven siblings. She met William Norris at a social, and they married in 1903. William died before I was born, but his wife was a one-foot-in-front-of-the-other kind of woman.

She had her appointed rounds, which she went on every day, always without stress, fuss, or hurry. She read her Bible, and after Roosevelt brought electricity to rural areas, voted Democratic. Grammy didn't mumble or mutter to herself, but often made a sound somewhere between a sigh and a ho-hum. The habit, which went with her wherever she went, may have come from living alone for so long.

A few days after I arrived, I settled into a routine of many choices but few chores. I woke each morning to the vigorous crow of a proud rooster. I rose from my blanket bed on the floor, where I slept next to Grammy's bed, and tumbled downstairs to the kitchen. Grammy would already be up and, even on hot days, had a fire going in the wood stove. Before breakfast I headed out to the chicken coop. The rooster had awakened the hens, who were ready when I opened their small ground-level door. Out they came, dozens of expectant and tentative White Leghorns. They tilted their heads and looked at me, surprised and curious, as though they'd never seen such a sight, even though I let them out every day. (Whoever says chickens are dumb knows what he is talking about.) The hens stepped carefully at first, then broke into a trot, heads down, to begin their day-long search for bugs, ants, and other edibles.

Every morning I took to the coop a basket and a stick. After opening the little door I lifted the lids that covered the nests and interrupted the reverie of a few stay-behind hens. They could tell no good was coming. Calm eyes turned glaring, and sharp beaks poised to peck my hand. Enter the stick. With it, I gently urged them off the nests. (For many years Grammy and I had a running argument. Since I'd sometimes find two eggs underneath, I was convinced that a hen could lay several a day. Grammy assured me that each bird could lay only one. At some point it occurred to me a hen could lay an egg and leave the nest and another hen could take its place. Grammy didn't need to be told that she was right. She had lived on a farm all her life. When challenged by the young city slicker she'd sometimes say, "Don't get too big for your britches.")

Occasionally I'd look out during the day and not see a single hen until my eyes searched under the trees. A glance at the sky would reveal what they'd seen: a circling hawk. At least chickens knew when to hide.

But they couldn't hide from Grammy. Fried chicken was the centerpiece of many noon dinners. We always ate mashed potatoes and potato rolls. Everyone remembered these potato rolls. Grammy made them without a recipe, and they always came out tender and delicious. We smothered them with fresh butter and chokecherry jam made from berries that grew on bushes around the farm. Sliced onions and cucumbers in diluted vinegar were as close as we got to a salad, but nearby would be a plate of sliced tomatoes. I enjoyed corn, peas, and green beans in season, and along with everyone else, a cold glass of iced tea. At one end of the table sat a tempting apple pie or two—a reminder to save room for dessert.

After dinner Grammy would wash the dishes, then settle into her black leather rocking chair in the sitting room. Her apron still on, a fly swatter across her lap, she'd unfold the *Nebraska State Journal*. Soon I'd hear a modest snore accompanying the whir of an electric fan in the hot afternoon.

One thing I remember about those summers is that Grammy let me be. Absent were parents' attempts to guide, mold, shape, and teach. The farm meant fresh air and freedom. There were few shoulds, don'ts, musts, and ought-tos. I could roam at will, do as I wanted, and it felt safe. Grammy had only two don'ts that I remember: "Don't lean too far back in that black leather chair, you'll break it," and "Don't bang the front porch swing against the outside of the house." The closest I came to forbidden fruit that she didn't know about was heading into the cornfield to smoke dried corn silk.

Besides corn and alfalfa, which Grammy raised to feed the cattle and pigs, five milk cows played a big part in life on the farm. At about 5 P.M. every day, I crossed the field of sorghum south of the house, stooped through a barbed-wire fence, and began to walk to their pasture. It was much smaller than an adjacent one of about six hundred acres that held the main herd. My chore was to bring the milk cows back to the barn. The long, narrow pasture was criss-crossed by trails etched deep into the earth. Grammy said they'd been made years earlier by buffalo. Looking ahead and to one side I could see the pastures' undulating hills. My mother said they'd once been home to hundreds of wild daisies and a huge colony of prairie dogs. But no more. To the north were corn and alfalfa fields and the wide green valley of the Republican River.

In 1969 I joined other family members for Grammy's funeral in Inavale and burial in the Red Cloud cemetery. She died in her ninety-fifth year. At the time it all felt matter-of-fact, but several years later, her death hit home. My cherished memories and the unspoken love between us stirred deep inside me. Once I questioned my mother about the wisdom of leaving a three-year-old on the farm. She said, "But your grandmother wanted you there very much. After my father died, you were not only named after him but also filled an important place in her life."

Not long ago I decided I had to have an old Burlington Route timetable. With the deaths of my twin aunt and uncle at the age of ninety-five— they'd grown up on the farm with their sister, my late mother—I was the one person left who knew how the farm operated when it was still run by the Norris family. The timetable would be an echo of my past.

For me, the desire to own stuff ebbs with age. However, I wanted that Burlington timetable. I wanted it because of what had happened on most nights on the front porch of the farmhouse. Grammy sat in her chair, I on the porch swing. We never said much. We listened to the sounds of crickets and frogs down by the creek, watched the flash of fireflies, looked at the stars, and heard the far-off benediction of a mourning dove. If one of us chanced to look north at just the right time—out over the corn fields and past the Republican River—we would see, ever so briefly, the distant light of a train just after it left Inavale on its way to Red Cloud. I knew the train belonged to the Burlington. I never thought about where it had come from, who rode on it, or where it was going. But I remembered its far-off, flickering light. I remembered those nights on the porch with Grammy. I wanted the timetable.

I searched for one on eBay. For $9.99 plus $2.00 shipping and handling, I bought a 1944 Burlington timetable from Tom Farley in West Orange, New Jersey. It was dog-eared in one corner and had two small tears along an edge. The cover was black and white and off-red. In the middle was a drawing of the Zephyr, a Burlington Streamliner. The phrases "Burlington Route," "Timetables," "Way of the Zephyrs," "America's Distinctive Trains," and, at the very bottom, "Corrected to April 9, 1944," appeared. I imagine it once belonged in a conductor's black satchel, traveled to places that I'd never seen, and could tell stories I'd never know.

I looked for "Inavale" in the table of contents. On page twenty I found table 6, "Kansas City–St. Joseph–Denver." That's what I was looking for: Train #32, a daily, passed through Inavale at 9:31 P.M. It was this train's light that Grammy and I saw from the porch. Beside "Inavale" was an italicized *f* indicating that the town was just a flag stop. Number 32 stopped only if flagged by the stationmaster. I learned that the train left Wray, Colorado, at 12:15 P.M., and somewhere between McCook and Indianola, Nebraska, it changed from Mountain to Central Standard Time. The small towns of Bartley, Arapahoe, Alma, Naponee, and Riverton lay ahead, and then Inavale.

After passing Inavale the train chugged on for seven miles to Red Cloud, where it stopped from 9:45 P.M. to 9:50 P.M., perhaps to change crews and take on water for the engine. Then it steamed eastward through Guide Rock, Superior, Chester, Wymore, Pawnee, and Rulo, crossed the Missouri River, and reached Kansas City at 7:20 A.M. In twenty hours, the train traveled five hundred miles.

I never rode the train or knew anyone who did. All I saw was a glimpse of its light. Grammy told me, though, that years earlier, when it was time to sell cattle, my grandfather would herd them on foot to Inavale, put them on board a train, and accompany the cattle to Kansas City. "And," she added, "he would come home in the caboose, very tired."

Though my mother said she never saw her parents show affection for each other, Grammy kept her husband's picture on her dresser. He died of a heart attack. According to Grammy, he lay down on the couch after lunch one day and never got up. Years later I found an obituary that said she'd found him dead one morning in the kitchen, feet warming on the door of the wood stove. I once asked my aunt which story was correct. She replied, "The newspaper."

Every summer, when the bus stopped in front of the McFarland Hotel in Red Cloud and I got off, Grammy and Uncle John were waiting in the Chevrolet coupe. I can see John grinning and imagine Grammy and me having a quick hug. I wasted no time running next door to the office of the *Commercial Advertiser,* the area's biweekly newspaper. In the next issue readers would find a small item: "Billy Buffett, son of Mr. and Mrs. Fred W. Buffett of Omaha, arrived on Thursday to spend the summer with his grandmother, Mrs. W. H. Norris of Inavale." It was now official. The summer could begin.

Six decades have passed since those boyhood summers. In 1992 much of the farm blew away in a tornado; the house still stands, as does the old chicken coop and a once-red shed. Gone are the windmills, a grain elevator, the outhouse, the milking barn, and the old cottonwood trees that lined the lane to the mailbox. The farm is still a working farm, rented to the second generation of a family named Hirsch. Inavale no longer boasts a post office. Surrounded by weeds, the old train station is boarded up and beaten down. The remains of tracks are rusted. Most of the ties have fallen away and rotted.

Inevitably the world moves on, but for me certain images from long ago are more vivid than the events of yesterday. I can see the porch, and Grammy, and the light of the train. The timetable reminds me of what once was real, of things that happened, of places that are no more, of people long gone, and of where I was at a particular time and place: in the summer at the farm, on the porch, at 9:31 P.M.

Siamese Moths

One morning on the playground during recess I saw them: two joined-together moths. "Siamese!" I thought and, carrying them carefully in my palm, ran to the principal's office of Beals School, where I was a third-grader. Miss Rassmussen heard my excitement as I asked her if I could call the local newspaper, the *Omaha World Herald*. I knew I'd found something of interest, probably worthy of a national feature in Ripley's Believe It Or Not.

Miss Rassmussen helped me dial the newspaper office. I told my story to the person who answered, suggesting they send a photographer. He agreed, saying that one would arrive soon. Shortly after I hung up, the moths came apart. Miss Rassmussen, bless her, knew I was too young to understand what the moths were up to, but she had nurtured my excitement and let me contact the paper. I called to tell them that the moths had come apart. They needn't send a photographer after all.

Remembering the incident now, I feel grateful for Miss Rassmussen's response. She could easily have brushed off my request or turned it into a pedantic learning experience. My appreciation stayed with me. When I got home on the afternoon of April 12, 1945, and learned of Franklin Delano Roosevelt's death, I wanted to tell someone important this important news. I called Miss Rassmussen.

apple crisp

I stopped by the Mohawk Orchard near Colrain, Massachusetts on a fall day in 1978. *The Apple Cookbook,* a paperback I hadn't seen before, was for sale. I asked the lady behind the counter to name its most praised recipe and right away she said, "The apple crisp recipe on page 172." I'll add my praise. I've made it many times, and no one has ever sent it back. It's especially good when made with a combination of Granny Smith and Golden Delicious apples.

ingredients:

4 cups apples, pared and sliced
2 tablespoons water
¾ cup sugar, divided
1½ cups biscuit mix
½ teaspoon cinnamon
1 egg
¼ cup melted butter

method:

Preheat oven to 400° F.

1. Grease an 8 in. square pan. Arrange the apples in the pan and sprinkle them with the water and ¼ cup of the sugar.

2. In a medium bowl, stir together the biscuit mix, ½ cup of the sugar, and the cinnamon. Beat the egg thoroughly; pour slowly into the dry mixture, stirring constantly with a fork until crumbly.

3. Sprinkle mixture over the apples and pour the butter evenly over the top. Bake for about 25 minutes or until brown. Serve warm or cold with ice cream or milk. (Note: For the biscuit mixture I use Bisquick.)

The Dishtowel

When I was a young boy the first small-screened black-and-white television sets began appearing in American homes. One of my favorite dramas was *I Led Three Lives,* the story of Herb Philbrick—family man, government agent, and Communist.

Our minds sometimes make strange connections. Recently, mine related an unusual dishtowel lying on my kitchen table to the triple identities of Herb Philbrick—the dishtowel has also led three lives.

In its first life and longest period of active service, the towel hung on a hook in the kitchen of my grandmother's farm. My great grandfather had homesteaded there, in Nebraska, near the Republican River, and on his farm my mother and her siblings were born. By the time I visited, the farm had grown to a thousand acres. When Grammy died, my mother took a stack of dishtowels, including the one that's now on my kitchen table, to our family home in Omaha and eventually to our cabin in western Massachusetts. In its second life of more than twenty years, the dishtowel sat unused on a back shelf.

Recently, I've had a renaissance of interest in my past. Thanks to my mother, who saved so much, I now possess quite a few artifacts from the farm. A hand-held implement owned by my great grandfather and used to plant corn, one seed at a time, hangs on my home office wall in Boston. Another wall features a still life painting of a bowl and various fruits that hung in the dining room of the old farmhouse. Now in its third incarnation, the dishtowel, when not in use, lies folded in a drawer with other towels.

I first saw this towel in 1936 when I traveled from our family home in Omaha to my grandmother's farm. The towel, or one like it, always hung in the kitchen. Cut from a heavy muslin sugar sack and hemmed on four sides by my grandmother on a sewing machine with a foot treadle, the towel is neither delicate nor particularly soft.

The towel dried the hands of my grandmother, who took over the farm when her husband died. It dried the hands of hired men, who would come in from the fields for dinner, and my Aunt Willa's delicate hands when she spent vacations on the farm. The towel also dried my hands and those of countless others.

Everybody washed their hands at the kitchen sink with rainwater from a buried cistern just outside the back porch. I learned early that this water wasn't for drinking. While cleaning out the cistern, Uncle John had once found a dead snake. The hand-washing ritual never varied. One of the hired men, Harold Smith, perhaps, would come from the back porch through a screen door and into the kitchen. To the left stood the sink and, attached to it, a hand pump. Above the sink sat a bar of Ivory soap. A few up and downs of the pump's handle and water flowed into the basin: wet the hands, take the soap, scrub a bit, rinse, then head for the towel in the corner.

Once his hands were dry, Harold moved into the dining room, ready to sit down and take a piece of fried chicken, some mashed potatoes, and other vegetables. When company came or during the harvest, up to eight people sat around the table, passing platters of food and, at the end of the meal, lifting a forkful of fresh-baked apple pie.

The towel was one of many things that stayed the same year after year, along with the wood box next to the stove, the flies hovering outside the screen door, the oppressive heat of the summer sun, and, of course, my grandmother. I took them for granted, as I did the cottonwood trees that lined the lane, the big barn where Uncle John milked the cows twice a day, and the rich soil in which good foods grew. I thought they would last forever.

Drying one's hands was, for me, a thoughtless activity, no match for heading out to a wire-enclosed coop for pullets, or half-grown chickens. I'd snatch one in my hands and carry it to a stump next to the woodpile, where my grandmother waited with the axe and a pail of hot water. Without fanfare, she raised the axe and cut off its head: routine for her, high drama for me. The headless bird went onto the woodpile, where its last spasms played out. After a plunge into hot water to make its feathers pluckable, the chicken went to the kitchen, where my grandmother lit some newspaper and singed off the pinfeathers. More than sixty years later I still remember every detail of that task. Looking at the towel reminds me.

Drying one's hands lacked the cachet of mounting a horse—either Doll or Dan—near the end of the day and riding into the pasture to fetch the milk cows. A dishtowel lacked the drama of the chalk cliffs overlooking the farm and the Republican River valley. For many hours I'd climb around, imagining a herd of buffalo ambling down the bluffs to drink water from the river. Sometimes I'd conjure up Indians walking by as they had done one day when my grandfather was a baby.

Though I remember the ritual, I don't actually recall drying my hands. There was so much else to enjoy. Every Tuesday afternoon and Saturday night we drove to Red Cloud, where I eagerly headed for the theater, gave Mrs. Beam my dime, bought a bag of popcorn from her husband, and settled into the auditorium for a double feature that might include films with Charlie Chan, Gene Autry, Abbott and Costello, Sherlock Holmes, and the Lone Ranger. I saw them all. The movies over, I'd head down Main Street to Mr. Hawley's drug store, hop on a stool, and dive into one of his butterscotch sundaes.

Drying hands was the dishtowel's only purpose. Today an item with the same task would be called a hand towel, suggesting something small and soft, which the farm towels weren't. This piece of cloth still bears marks from a long life of service—some remnant of dirt or grease or oil or soot overlooked on hands that tilled the soil, cooked on a wood stove, or played in the dirt. Mysterious smudges are part of the dishtowel's past. And there are marks made by an iron used to press the towel. In the days before electricity, my grandmother carried a hot iron from the wood stove to the ironing board with a gripper handle. When that iron lost its heat, Grammy would take it to the stove, detach the handle, and clamp on a hot one. If the iron was too hot or her attention flagged, the iron left a rust-colored stain—still visible today.

The towel's provenance still shows in faded blue lettering:

C and H Sugar

California and Hawaiian Sugar Refining Corporation

San Francisco, California

MANUFACTURER

100 Lbs Net, 10–10's

In the middle, surrounded by red lines are these words:

Pure Cane—Berry Granulated

The towel is still sturdy and still bears the blotches that testify to its life on a Nebraska farm. It will surely outlast me. Someday, when I'm gone, somebody else will unfold the muslin artifact. My hope is that it will be a child or a grandchild, a kid who has never heard of the three lives of Herb Philbrick or about drying hands washed with water from a cistern. I hope the child will pick the towel up and ask, "What's this?" And an appreciative parent who has read this tale will say, "This is a dishtowel with stories to tell."

Once a Ringmaster

Though it isn't on my résumé, I was the ringmaster of Miss Reynolds's second-grade circus at Beals Elementary School in Omaha. The year was 1940, and I was seven. I don't remember whether I volunteered or was appointed. Being a ringmaster happened only once. It came early in life, when running the show required very little. I never was ringmaster again—as a CEO, a general, or a coach.

Our circus offered no competition to Ringling Brothers Barnum and Bailey, and we never became wild like today's media circuses. We had no future, not because we weren't good but because Miss Reynolds had other projects for us.

Our circus offered three performances: one for our school, one for the PTA, and one for Pickard, an elementary school near Beals. For one afternoon, we were a traveling circus.

There were three acts. In a booming voice, I announced the opening routine: "Ladies and gentlemen, our first act features the amazing tightrope walker, Gilbert Davis." Larry Sutter and Jimmie Olsen, two of our classmates, held the rope. All was ready. Gilbert motioned to his assistants to lower the rope a bit. This continued until it lay on the floor. Then, with great care and a look of fear, Gilbert walked the rope. I remember wild applause.

Next came our strongman. "Billy Winstrom, the strongest young man in the Midwest," I hollered, extending my arm in greeting. An apparently heavy barbell lay before him. With boyish groans and brute strength, Billy raised it to his waist, then, with more effort, above his head. The applause was thunderous. After Billy exited, Annie Dinkel, the smallest girl in our class, appeared on stage and skipped off, carrying the barbell.

Finally, to bring the greatest show at Beals to a stirring close, on walked Adrienne Rice. "And now, ladies and gentlemen, from distant shores, the world-famous mind reader, Madame Latonka!" While I blindfolded her, the audience studied her gypsy costume. I walked into the audience, held up someone's wrist, and asked in a commanding voice, "Madame Latonka, can you tell what I'm touching? Now watch out." With furrowed brow and intense concentration, a confident Madame Latonka said, "A watch." Jaws dropped.

Again I approached the audience and held up a hand. "Madame, what am I looking at right now? I hope this rings a bell." More furrowed brows, more concentration, and then finally, "A ring." The applause was deafening.

Billy Winstrom stayed in Omaha and went into the oil business. Jimmy, now Jim, became a high school teacher, as did I, and lives in California. I've known him since kindergarten and we still correspond—we've been good friends for seventy years. Gilbert joined the Air Force, became a test pilot, and too early in life, was killed in a crash.

I heard from Adrienne several years ago. She became a wife, a mother, and more. I remember that she came over to my house to play, and I went over to hers. How long did our relationship continue? A little longer than the circus.

My mother saved photos from the circus and put them in a scrapbook. Beside one of the pictures she wrote: "The Ringmaster for the PTA Show. He was a grand one too. Mother so proud of him."

Our lives unfolded. Some paths we walked were more difficult than others. There was no one to lower the rope. Some weights we carried really were heavy. And, when we had to make guesses in our lives, no one gave us hints. We had to watch out, often with no cheers. Perhaps, though, our performance was good training in what psychologists today call positive reinforcement. Our little second-grade circus enjoyed resounding success.

peach dumplings

I include this recipe not only because it is a treasured family recipe, but also in honor of my brother Fred C. Buffett, who died of a rare form of kidney cancer in November, 1997, a few days after his 61st birthday. Of all the things my mother made, this was his favorite.

1½ cups flour
3 teaspoons Royal Baking Powder
½ teaspoon salt
5 tablespoons shortening
½ cup milk
6 peaches, canned or fresh
(if canned, reserve liquid for sauce)
6 tablespoons sugar

Preheat the oven to 400°.

1. Sift together flour, baking powder and salt; rub shortening in lightly; add just enough milk to make a soft dough.

2. Roll the dough one-eighth inch thick on a lightly floured board. Divide it into six equal parts. Lay on each a peach that has been pared. Sprinkle it with sugar, moisten the edges of the dough, and fold it around the peach, pressing the edges tightly together.

3. Place in a large greased baking pan; sprinkle with sugar and put a piece of butter on top of each dumpling.

4. Pour sauce around dumplings (recipe follows) and bake about forty minutes.

sauce:

Juice from one can of halved peaches
½ cup white sugar
½ cup brown sugar
grated rind and juice of 1 lemon
3 tablespoons unsalted butter

Pour the peach liquid into a two-cup graduate. Add enough water to make two cups of liquid. Cook the first 4 ingredients in a heavy saucepan over low heat, stirring occasionally, until the sugar dissolves. Increase the heat and bring to a boil until reduced. Remove from heat and stir in the butter.

Makes six dumplings.

Home on Hickory Street

My mother, father, and I moved to Hickory Street in 1937, when I was four and my brother Fred, called Fritz, was on the way. Our little white bungalow on Williams Street, six blocks to the north, was no longer big enough. Made of brick, the Hickory Street house was part of an all-white, middle-class neighborhood that extended for many blocks. The house stayed in our family until my mother died in 2004, sixty-seven years after she'd moved in.

There were children in the neighborhood. My brother and I could walk to our elementary school and later took public buses to our high school near downtown Omaha. Both schools still stand, and I'm still friends with a few people from both places.

The McBrides lived across the street and down the hill. They had a long, flat driveway perfect for games of "Mother, May I?" I haven't heard this game mentioned in decades. "Mother" stood at the finish line, and all the players faced her at the starting line. A player would ask, "Mother, may I take two giant steps forward?" Mother would either grant permission or say, "No, you may take three baby steps backward." Mother would tell each child how many baby, scissor, or giant steps he or she could take. The first kid to reach the finish line got to be the next mother. Did we realize how easily Mother could manipulate the results? A player could try to sneak towards the finish, but if Mother caught you, it was back to the starting line.

The house west of the McBrides' belonged to the Thompsons, and it was there, one morning when I was of tender years, that I came of age.

Shirley and I were sitting on her living room couch when, without prelude, warning, or fanfare, she pulled down her panties and said, "Wanna touch?" I like to think that my hand was on the way when we heard the footsteps of the cleaning lady coming from the kitchen. The hand retreated, the panties rose, and innocence returned, sort of.

The Teasers lived two houses east of us. Mister Teaser owned a Bohemian meat market in South Omaha that his son Johnny, the neighborhood bully, eventually inherited. Johnny played a key role in the only spanking I ever got from my dad. Now, I had an uncle who three times was elected to Congress from Nebraska's First District. Prior to the elections a "Buffett for Congress" sign stood in our front yard. One night I reported it missing and, when asked, said that I'd seen Johnny Teaser grab it and run home.

Father called Mr. Teaser and learned that Johnny had been home all evening. Hand in hand, my father and I headed to the basement. This was the first and only time I ever heard the words, "This is going to hurt me more than it will you." It didn't hurt me at all, and I don't imagine it hurt him very much, either. I don't know why I lied, but it was probably to pay Johnny back for bullying me. I wouldn't have dared to slug him. He was older and stronger, and I had a wimpy streak.

Between our house and the Teasers lived the Stilmocks, the only couple on the block that was both odd and childless. Ethel was short and heavy and appeared to amble around the house every day in slippers and a patched housecoat. Only twice did I see her dressed up and stepping into a taxi. She and Mother were occasional across-the-driveway friends, and later, Ethel sold or gave my mother her silver tableware, never used by my mother. The silver still rests in its mahogany box in our basement, a formal S etched in the handle of every piece.

Ethel's husband Judie, whose name now reminds me of the Johnny Cash song "A Boy Named Sue," owned a tavern in South Omaha. Cut from the same cloth as the bully Johnny, Judie looked and talked as if he was ready anytime to grab a miscreant and toss him into the street. I had another reason to stay on his good side: he paid me to shovel snow from his driveway, wanting it clear before he got home from work.

One fall afternoon another fellow and I were tossing a football in Judie's driveway. One of us missed, and the ball sailed through a pane of glass in his garage door. The door was locked.

I waited for Judie to come home and explained that if he'd just open the door, I'd gladly sweep up the broken glass. He declined but assured me he'd take care of it. True to his word, he did. The next morning I found the glass scattered in our backyard.

Jimmy Buckley, who lived in the house just west of ours, was probably the boy I was playing catch with. He was my best friend in the neighborhood, though he went to the local Catholic school. I still have a photo of the two of us peering out of a snow house we'd made in my backyard for secret meetings. In the summer his mom frequented the horse races at Ak-Sar-Ben—Nebraska spelled backwards—and all year long his dad spent ever longer hours at a tavern on nearby Center Street. Jimmy later became The Honorable James F. Buckley, a judge in the Douglas County court system.

Fritz and I shared a room on the second floor on the west side of the house. When we were young, Mother used to storm in, yardstick in hand, and pound the covers to quiet us down. My brother and I played a game called face tag, which involved catching the other's eye, putting up a hand, saying "Face tag," and looking away quickly. We occasionally "touched tongues" and then cringed in disgust. A fonder memory of mine is lying in the dark with a little crystal set I'd sent for in reponse to a comic book promotion. If I tilted both my head and the radio just right, I could just about pick up a broadcast of the Omaha Knights hockey team.

Nothing really bad ever happened in our house. The worst thing I remember is hearing my mother cry out from the kitchen and arriving to find her on the floor, blood spurting from her wrist. She'd been using a metal appliance to squeeze juice when the handle broke and punctured her vein.

Though I'd outgrown Boy Scouts, I remembered my training and applied a textbook tourniquet to her upper arm. We got into the car and went to the emergency room of a nearby hospital. Medical personnel took over, and when my bandaged mother emerged I awaited the nurse's praise for my tourniquet. None was offered, so I asked. "Oh, it was fine," she replied nonchalantly, "but next time you can just do this," calmly placing her thumb over an imaginary puncture on my arm.

The house was governed by a comfortable routine. My father worked six days a week from 4:30 A.M. until 6 P.M. He'd come home; I'd get his slippers, take off his shoes, and fetch him a beer. I always got a sip.

Because he got up early and often snored, my parents slept in separate rooms. One night I got home late from a date and surprised the two of them in bed together. I suppressed any thought of this being unusual or cause for wonder. My mother fixed dinners, mended our socks, belonged to P.E.O., and took long walks for exercise. At some point my parents gave up going out on Saturday nights because they were too sleep-deprived on Sunday morning. We always went to church.

My first date was in second or third grade, when I took a schoolmate and neighbor, Sally Neevel, to the Boy Scout circus. I also hosted a party in our basement. It was there that Patsy Evers, the class heartthrob, received her first spin-the-bottle kiss behind a curtain. I wish I were sure that I'd won and that it was my virginal lips that brushed hers behind that curtain. Now Pat Waller, she still lives in her original home on Williams Street.

The morning after high school graduation, our house was the last stop of a progressive party that ended with my folks providing breakfast. My father had created a hand-painted sign that looked just like the ones he put in the grocery store window advertising a sale on bananas or canned peaches. This one read, "Through This Door Pass the Smartest People in the World."

Three months later I left the house at 4515 Hickory Street for college, returning only for vacations and later, accompanied by my wife and children, to visit my parents. Hickory Street slowly faded as the center of my life.

After my father died and my mother got much older, I visited her often. She could no longer travel. I was with her when she died in the house, on the night of August 17, 2004. Also with her were my wife Susan, my mother's niece, Susan Buffett, and my mother's longtime caretaker, Helen Perea.

About six months before her end, I learned from Helen that some attorneys were there with papers for my mother to sign. With no evidence, but with fearful stories about aging dowagers being bilked of their money, I got nervous and upset with my mother. When I called her later—we talked often—I learned that she was adding Helen to her will. As a result, Helen inherited enough money to buy 4515 after my mother died.

For five years Helen and her family have been living there. Helen, who is Hispanic, is a saint to the core; five pictures of my mother grace the walls of Helen's home. She notes gratefully: "Now we don't have to worry about waking up in the morning and finding our tires slashed."

My mother's last good deed—integrating the neighborhood.

most likely to succeed

dummy pages

levi's

white polka dots

video camera

hi-y club

spanish moss

colored chalk

first methodist

louis the sixteenth

guillotine

superglue

road to damascus

general electric

greyhound bus

oh, for gosh sakes

saxophone

louis armstrong

third davis

bisquick and milk

fire escape

bald spot

meadowlarks

afterbirth

morning mouth

HOME AND BEYOND

a good joe

ymca

box office

detention

jumpy stomach

greek blacksmith

temple of apollo

liver

cottage cheese

watermelon

mount rushmore

rodgers and hammerstein

horn-rimmed glasses

mechanical drawing

class e hotel

sheep bells

sox dance

midwest conference

broadway

shubert theater

dark suits

stage door

belgian congo

sly tricks

ring finger

tambourine

spare ribs

rutabaga

cunard liner

threshing floor

streetlights

clay jug

kerosene lamp

wooden tub

turkish coffee

hard-boiled eggs

en donkeys

sprig of thyme

A Lingering Headline

Remember those senior-year awards in high school—Best Athlete, Best-Looking, Most Likely to Succeed, Friendliest? I never won any of those but was named Best Journalist. It was awarded automatically to the editor of the Central High newspaper, who was chosen by Anne Lane Savage, the paper's advisor and Central's journalism teacher.

Thursday was the big day on the paper. The entire staff stayed after school to "put the paper to bed." Articles were laid out and headlines were written for each one. Later, we'd deliver dummy pages to the printer, and students received it the next day.

Three other fellows on the staff and I tried to give the paper a bit of notoriety by wearing Levi's every Thursday along with blue shirts with white polka dots and blue socks knit by our girlfriends. Few noticed, but we had fun.

I enjoyed being the editor, but the single memory I have from my tenure is unpleasant. One time the staff decided that the lead article would be about Central's upcoming Road Show, an annual occasion featuring several variety acts. The show was one of the year's big events.

I assigned a straight-A staff member, Peter Weil, to the article. It didn't take him long to return to my desk with his headline: "Weeks of Rehearsal Culminate in Four Performances."

"Not bad," I said. "But 'culminate' has to go."

He objected vigorously and took the issue to Mrs. Savage. She sided with him. "Culminate" stayed in.

Petty as it sounds, I never forgot the incident. Why? Was it because Mrs. Savage pulled rank? Was it because I'd never seen "culminate" in a headline and thought it too sophisticated for our paper? Was it because a complex word was used in place of a simpler one like "end"? I don't know. Do trees know why moss clings to them? Who knows why this memory clung to me?

When our class held its fiftieth reunion, the weekend ended with a dinner at a local country club. The few speeches were short; greeting old friends was the main activity. Some fellow with a video camera was there to capture our memories. Spotting Peter at a nearby table, I decided to tell my headline story. While we stood side by side and the camera rolled, I recounted the incident—the *Register,* Thursdays after school, the Road Show, his headline, my being overruled on "culminate," and my lasting pique. When I finished, Peter said, "What in the hell are you talking about?" He had no memory of the incident. The humorous apology I'd imagined never came.

I think of the incident rarely, but when I do I still feel a slight irritation. I don't blame Mrs. Savage, an excellent mentor, or Peter Weil, truly an innocent. I guess I just didn't like being overruled, and except for that time in the *Register,* I've never seen "culminate" in a headline.

chicken betty's fried chicken

I found this recipe many years ago in *The New York Times*. Chicken Betty, who was famous for her chicken, worked in several diners near Kansas City. When she changed establishments, loyal fans would follow her.

I've made this recipe probably fifteen times over the years. Though labor-intensive, it always gets raves. For some it is the first home-fried chicken they've ever tasted.

chicken:

1 frying chicken, 3 to 3¼ pounds

1 large egg

⅔ cup milk

2 cups flour

salt

ground black pepper

Accent brand seasoning mix (optional)

¾ to 1 cup lard

¾ to 1 cup solid vegetable shortening

1½ tablespoons salt

1 teaspoon monosodium glutamate (optional)

gravy:

2 scant tablespoons flour

2 to 3 cups milk, as needed

Salt and black pepper, to taste

1. Cut the chicken into nine pieces: a backbone, two thighs, two breasts, two drumsticks and two wings. Wash and dry each piece. Remove them from the refrigerator 20 to 30 minutes before frying.

2. Beat the egg with the milk in a wide bowl. Place the flour in a 9-inch by 13-inch baking pan. Add salt, pepper, and Accent, if using.

3. Heat ¾ cup lard and ¾ cup vegetable shortening in a 12-inch skillet, preferably cast iron.

4. Dip each piece of chicken in the egg mixture. Place the pieces on a plate or on waxed paper.

5. Turn the chicken, a few pieces at a time, in the flour until thoroughly coated.

6. Gently tap the floured pieces of chicken against each other to shake off excess flour. Place in the hot fat. Chicken pieces should not be crammed into the pan, but they can be fairly close. Fry chicken over moderately high heat until golden brown on one side, then turn and brown the second side. It should take about seven minutes to brown each side, so adjust the heat accordingly. When the chicken is golden brown on both sides, cover the pan about two-thirds of the way. Reduce heat so that frying continues steadily but gently for 15 to 18 minutes after covering the pan. Turn the pieces several times during that period, and lower the heat if the chicken browns too quickly. The final result should be a deep copper color without any hint of blackness. Add fat, if necessary, to keep the chicken "swimming."

7. Drain chicken on paper towels. Continue frying until all pieces are done. Keep fried pieces hot by placing them on a rack in an open baking pan in a preheated 250° oven.

8. To make gravy, discard the grease in your frying pan(s) but not the browned flour.

9. Place the pan over low heat until simmering; stir in flour. Sauté, stirring constantly for seven or eight minutes, or until flour browns and mixture is a thick paste. Pour in about one and one-half cups of milk. Whisk and simmer until smooth and fairly thick. Add salt and pepper to taste. The gravy should simmer for seven or eight minutes more. Add milk as necessary to achieve the consistency of heavy cream. Adjust seasonings; the gravy should be very peppery and a creamy cocoa brown in color.

10. Serve the chicken in a basket lined with paper napkins or towels and the gravy in a heated gravy boat. Spoon the gravy over homemade baking powder biscuits and/or stiff, buttery mashed potatoes, not over the chicken. Cole slaw provides a refreshing contrast in flavor and texture.

Serves two to three persons.

Note:

If you fry two chickens, use one jumbo egg and one cup milk, plus an extra cup of flour for dredging. All other ingredients can be doubled. If you use two pans for frying, keep the breasts in one and the thighs and drumsticks in the other. Giblets, wings, and backbones can be fried when other pieces are done, since they will cook thoroughly in about 10 minutes after they have browned.

Miss Clark's Discovery

As a young boy, I once entered a women's restroom by mistake. Six years later, I erred again, on the Thursday before Easter in 1951, at about 7:10 in the morning. This time it was in the First Methodist Church in Omaha, across the street from my high school.

The church felt deserted when I arrived early to lead a Lenten service. As an officer in the Hi-Y Club, I'd been assigned to preside over the event. (Hi-Y was affiliated with the YMCA.) The halls were quiet. I saw no one. I decided to use the bathroom before anyone arrived. A door marked "WOMEN" was to my left. I didn't see the one for men, and there wasn't a soul around. "Why not?" I thought.

I looked left and right again, went in, and locked the door of a stall. A minute later, footsteps! The door to the women's room opened! Panicked, I stood up, making sure my head was beneath the top of the stall. I couldn't see anyone through the thin crack at the door's edge, but after a pause, the door opened again, and the footsteps began to recede. Fearing their owner's return, I hurriedly finished and carefully stepped out. To my left the hall was clear, but to my right I saw the receding backside of my former World History teacher, Genevieve Clark. I tiptoed to the left and around the corner. Eventually, a small group gathered, and I led the service.

Later that day, between classes at school, I crossed paths with Miss Clark. "Say, Bill," she said, "you weren't by any chance in the women's restroom over at the church this morning, were you?"

"Oh, heavens, no!" I said with conviction. Why would she think a thing like that?

I don't remember if she said, "Well, I didn't think so," or if she simply walked away.

As far as the students were concerned, Miss Clark was a character. We decided she led Central's pantheon of eccentrics. Short, elderly, and wearing clothes that hung like Spanish moss, she presented a pale, wan face to the world. In winter, in big letters made with colored chalk, she wrote her seasonal admonition on the board: "FEED THE BIRDS."

She had a unique way of conducting class. Our nightly reading assignment provided fodder for the next day's quizzing. Miss Clark, sitting at her desk, textbook before her, might say, "Richard, a B for this one: 'Which king was known as the Sun King?'" If he didn't know, the question passed to the person behind him. When she heard a correct answer, she'd move on. "Sally, an A for this one: Who was the wife of Louis the Sixteenth?" And, "David, two A's for this: Name three leaders of the French Revolution."

Every day, week after week, with the exception of test days, this is how she taught class. She didn't record grades; that job belonged to Lora Lee Smith, a fellow student and Miss Clark's designated trustee.

Sometimes we got a break. Miss Clark possessed a large glass case in the back of the room filled with antiquarian objects; some were the real thing, others copies. Occasionally, she would stop the quizzing and show off something from her case. During our study of eighteenth-century France, a working model of a guillotine appeared. She yanked a string to demonstrate its sliding blade.

I had lucked out at the Methodist Church that Lenten morning, but not the day when the class tried to get her off the subject. "Where did you go to school?" someone asked. "Are you a native Nebraskan?" What was her favorite thing to do outside of school? Invariably we edged toward discovering her age, and naturally she declined to say; however, she readily told us how long she'd been teaching.

I popped the question. "How old were you when you started teaching?" Her tired eyes landed on me with a look of profound disappointment. "Bill," she said, "you go and sit behind the case." The case served not only as Miss Clark's Museum of History but also as a holding pen for miscreants. Finally the bell sounded, and students began to scramble out. Miss Clark approached. "Bill," she said, "you go home and tell your parents that they have a very ill-mannered son."

Since then I've never asked a woman her age, and I'll never again enter the women's room in an apparently deserted church, or anywhere else, for that matter.

Sweethearts

Recently I asked myself: "If I could go back in time for an hour or so and watch something I'd done in my past, what would it be?" I decided that I'd return to the fall of 1950, when I was seventeen and beginning my senior year at Central High in Omaha. I would sit in the audience of the school's annual operetta, Victor Herbert's *Sweethearts*. I'd go a second night if I could. I had a minor comic lead: Percy Algernon Slingsby, the Englishman. Alice Middlekauf sang the lead female role and Bill Burke, the lead male role. I've forgotten the plot and much else, but I haven't forgotten playing Percy.

Nor have I forgotten my moment in the sun: a solo called "I Don't Know How I Do It, But I Do." The title served as the first line. The lyrics continued, "I don't know how I've done it when it's done: I only know that I, have ready some reply whenever people cry. . . ." There were several more verses. I also remember the director, Elsie Howe Swanson, asking me to speak rather than sing my solo. I'd always assumed this was because I didn't have the voice for it, but not long ago an acquaintance sent me a copy of the original music. The instructions read, "Spoken."

During one rehearsal, at the end of the solo, I accidentally broke my cane over my knee. Fellow cast members laughed, so we decided I'd do it at each performance. Every night I'd glue my cane back together before going to bed. Fortunately (since this was before SuperGlue), there were no matinees.

Years ago I began to realize that there were important people in my past whom I'd never had a chance to thank. One was Ms. Swanson. "Swanie" was a demanding musician whose high standards were always evident. During one rehearsal, for example, Phil Abramson and I were horsing around. She glared at me and said, "I'm sorry I ever laid eyes on you." I'm sure I deserved it.

Alice Middlekauf and Bill Burke were an attractive and popular item offstage as well as on. Alice and I both ended up going to Carleton College. One night, early in our freshman year, she and I were dancing in a campus nightspot called The Cave. I remember only one moment. We were talking about our high school romances when she looked up and with dreamy eyes (I'm sure) said, "You're the only one I ever really cared about."

Ah, what we don't know in high school!

NIGHT TRAIN THROUGH INAVALE

THE DISHTOWEL

HOME ON HICKORY STREET

END OF MY ONLY SOLO (SPOKEN AT THAT) IF I DON'T KNOW HOW I DO IT BUT I DO! EACH NIGHT CAME WAS GLUED IN

SWEETHEARTS

CHECKER #74

Forgotten and Remembered

Your third-grade teacher's name, please. Who was your first kiss? What about the first bully you encountered? Your first movie? Something someone, anyone, said in high school? Do you recall any of these? So many things happen in a lifetime. Some we remember; many we don't. And some that profoundly alter our lives are later forgotten— even by those who played a major role.

Although I'll never match the Apostle Paul and his conversion on the road to Damascus, I did have a life-changing moment once, with similar suddenness and surprise. Afterwards, my life took off in a new direction. The incident happened in the spring of 1955 during my senior year at college. At the time, my friends all knew their career plans. My roommates, Phil and Don, were headed to seminary. I had no calling but had to do something. Without enthusiasm, I chose business. After several interviews, General Electric offered me a job, and I accepted. At least I had a place to report to after college.

Two weeks later, when I sat down to study in my dorm room, it happened. I never could explain how or why, but when I got up, I had a future, firm, clear, and unmistakable. I would become a teacher. The path lay straight in front of me, free of all my previous agonizing.

After breakfast the next morning, I headed over to Carleton's Placement Office and spoke with its director, Leith Shackel. "Leith," I said, "I have a confession to make: I don't want to go into business. I want to go into teaching." She smiled, eyes sparkling, and said, "I wondered when you were going to reach that decision. One man who interviewed you said that you should become a dean of men at some college. Another thought you belonged as headmaster of a boys' school. You're lucky. Some men fret and fume in business for two years before it hits them! Think of all the time you've saved."

I sent a letter of regret to General Electric and made an appointment to see Frank Kille, dean of the faculty. We had become friends after my election as president of the student government. During the next few days, he called a friend at the Yale University Graduate School of Education, and I was accepted into their Master of Arts in Teaching program with a Rockefeller Foundation scholarship.

That summer I boarded a Greyhound bus for New Haven, and I graduated from Yale the next spring. In the fall of 1956, I began teaching social studies at New Trier Township High School in Winnetka, Illinois.

In 1995, when my college class held its fortieth reunion, I asked around to see if Leith Shackel was still alive. She was. She and her partner, Jane Andrews, lived in a Northfield retirement community. I called and Jane answered.

"Jane, this is a voice out of the past."

"Who's this?"

"Bill Buffett."

"Oh, for gosh sakes."

Half an hour later I knocked at the door and Jane answered. Leith, clad in a white knit sweater with a comforter over her lap, sat in a wheelchair. Older, of course, but easily recognizable, they still had their sharp-edged vitality. We spoke of their many travels and their hopes of taking one more trip, to Alaska.

As I've gotten older, I've realized there are people who have helped me in life that I've never thanked adequately. So I told Leith how much

I valued her letting me come to the decision to teach on my own and not steering me away from business. She had trusted me to find my way, and I've been grateful ever since. She smiled, looked at me, and said, "I have no memory of that."

Amazing, I thought.

Since then I've thought more about the tricks memory plays. As a senior at Carleton, I was a proctor on Third Davis, a floor in the freshman dorm. My mother saved many of my letters home, in which I told stories about they guys who lived on the floor. Last year, the men who were freshmen that year had their fiftieth reunion and invited their old proctors back. Two of us made the trip.

I decided to excerpt from my letters a few stories about Third Davis and give them out at the reunion. Several tales concerned a student named Ted, who, though he had some neurological problems, finished the year. He never did graduate from Carleton. Music was and remains his passion, and he loyally returns to reunions, saxophone in hand.

I hoped to include in my handout several incidents about Ted but wanted his okay before adding them. We'd been out of touch for more than fifty years, but I found his name and number in the alumni directory. Voices change little over time. I recognized Ted's immediately.

"I still remember something you told me," he said, after we'd chatted for a while.

"What?" I asked.

"When I wasn't getting good grades, I asked you if I should give up saxophone. You said, 'Ted, would Louis Armstrong give up his trumpet?'"

Just as Leith had forgotten what she'd said, I had no memory of my remark to Ted.

Another encounter with memory occurred at the fiftieth reunion of the "Third Davis" men. I read an excerpt from one of my letters about a Sunday morning when they were freshmen and I was their proctor.

Dear Family,

What a beautiful day! Phil and I got up at 5:45 a.m. to introduce some of the guys to our famous early Sunday morning breakfasts. The sun was shining, the birds singing. What a super A double plus time we had. We could only talk eleven guys into getting up that early, and so with dates, we were twenty-two. What a crew. What a great time. Close to 6 a.m., Tom Blackburn stumbled into the room, mumbled "Ready, Buff," and sank into a chair.

We had bought all the food yesterday afternoon, but I had some Bisquick and milk that had to be mixed for making twists. With no bowl, we cleaned out our washbasin and dumped it all in, stirred it by hand, and shoved it all back into the box. I wish you could have seen our motley crew . . . most of them suffering from morning mouth, but once outside nobody was ailing.

The gals had to climb down the fire escape to get out of the dorm early— the doors didn't open until 7. We all met out on the bald spot, and it wasn't long before everyone got fully awakened. Off we trudged: food, big can of cocoa, and bricks to build the fireplace. North we headed, up by the farm, down a country road with meadowlarks singing. We walked by the pasture where a cow stood. She'd just birthed a calf the night before and it was still a little wet. Though the afterbirth wasn't too appetizing a sight before breakfast, our mature college group handled it well. The little calf was hunting around for its first breakfast. Mother's udder was huge. Shapiro observed, "There's plenty there if he can only find it."

On we went. This beautiful spot is about a mile from campus. We had bacon, eggs, orange juice, sweet rolls, twists, and hot cocoa, all so good! And everything was ready on time: hot bacon, hot eggs, and hot cocoa. After we ate, some of us had to go back for church, but the rest stopped at the farm. Some guys climbed the water tower. Several of us went into the barn. Here was a big old bull with a ring in its nose, some calves about two weeks old, the smell of old silage, and over in the corner, a cat with five kittens born about a week ago. . . .

At least six of the men attending the reunion in 2008 had been on that Sunday breakfast excursion. What surprises me is that not one of us remembered it. Perhaps others did, but not those at the reunion. For us, the event lives on only in the letter I'd written to my family fifty years earlier.

Three incidents: my remembering something Leith had forgotten, not recalling something Ted had never forgotten, and everyone forgetting a stellar event on a fine spring morning. In order for any event to become what we think of as history, someone must be a witness. That person must remember and then must either record it or tell it to someone who will. Finally, the record must survive and come to light. We can study the past, both our own and that of civilization, but we'll never know what-all we're missing.

all-american chili

This is a favorite of ours. I came across it one day in *Cooking Light* and have made it many times. It tastes even better the second day, and as a bonus, it freezes well.

6 oz. hot turkey sausage

2 cups chopped onion

1 cup chopped green pepper

1 lb. ground sirloin

1 jalapeño pepper, chopped

2 tablespoons chili powder

2 tablespoons brown sugar

1 tablespoon ground cumin

3 tablespoons tomato paste

1 teaspoon dried oregano

2 bay leaves

1 teaspoon ground black pepper

½ teaspoon salt

1¼ cups red wine

2 ea. 28-oz. cans diced tomatoes

2 ea. 15-oz. cans kidney beans, drained

½ cup reduced-fat sharp cheddar cheese

1. Place a large Dutch oven over medium-high heat. Remove casings from sausage. Add sausage, onion, pepper, sirloin, and jalapeño to pot; cook 8 minutes, or until sausage and beef are browned, stirring to crumble.

2. Add chili powder, brown sugar, cumin, tomato paste, oregano, bay leaves, black pepper, and salt. Cook for one minute. Stir in wine, tomatoes, and kidney beans. Bring to a boil, cover, reduce heat, and simmer 1 hour, stirring occasionally.

3. Uncover and cook for 30 minutes, stirring occasionally. Discard bay leaves. Sprinkle each serving with shredded cheese.

Yield: 8 servings.

The Perfect Season

On a Saturday afternoon in the fall of 1954, I trudged up the hill from Carleton's football stadium to Laird Hall. Our undefeated Knights had just won their sixth straight game. With one game left, we seemed certain to end our season without a loss, and, as president of the Carleton Student Association, I had a question for the dean of the faculty, Frank Kille. He was sitting behind his desk when I walked in. "Dean," I said, "as I'm sure you know, Ripon College is a pretty poor team. If our guys finish the season undefeated, could we take a day off school?"

Kille was a short man of average build. He wore glasses and sported a bow tie, and though he acted and talked in a deliberate way common to academics, there was always a ready twinkle in his eyes.

He leaned back, folded his hands under his chin, and said, "Well, if you want my honest opinion, I think it's a poor idea. I've been anticipating a request like this. It's what colleges usually do. I wonder if Carleton could be different. Why stop progress in one field, the academic, to celebrate progress in another, athletics? Next spring when the Phi Beta Kappas are announced, should we cancel a baseball game? Taking a day off school is a lazy man's way. Why not think of something creative, something that takes a little more imagination?"

With that unassailable argument, we began to talk. The main idea came from him. "When the team returns next week," he said, "let's have a celebration. We'll forget about curfews in the female dorms and have the faculty serve a supper." (At Carleton in the fifties, the women had to be in their dorms by twelve on Saturday nights.) Over the next few days, a small committee and I arranged the details.

Looking through old files recently, I found a yellow mimeographed flyer outlining the coming festivities:

To All Members of Carleton College—
Students, Faculty and Administration:

What: Gala Football Victory Celebration
Where: Carleton College
When: Saturday Night—11:45 p.m. til ????

Here is a schedule of events:

A. Bus Arrival: *The football bus will arrive about midnight. Everyone should be out on the Bald Spot by 11:45 p.m.. If you are going to the formal you'll have to leave early to change clothes. The bus will enter the campus by Gridley and proceed around the Bald Spot to the gym. The route will be lined with some 80 to 100 torches. A giant flare is being built by the Chemistry Department and will be exploded on the Bald Spot. The main part of the student body will greet the team at the gym. The band will be there. Each team member's picture will be taken as he steps off the bus. While the bus is unloading, fifteen aerial bombs will be set off on the Bald Spot. After the team is off the bus everyone will proceed into the gym.*

B. Gym Show: *This will be a football victory show. It will be a fast ... all star ... thirty minute show. Even members of the faculty and adminis-tration will be present to participate.*

C. Sox Dance: *After the show there will be a dance in the gym. All on record ... in your sox ... much fun!* Date or Non Date *... either way.*

D. Tea Room: *Also after the show the Tea Room will be open where Clarence and members of the faculty and administration will serve a real football victory spread. Food for everyone!*

E. Union: *The Union will be open ... fire in the fire place ... card playing.*

These are the essentials. There are other details. We hope this will be the greatest celebration in Carleton's history. Bands, sirens, bells, torches, flares, fireworks, show, food served by the faculty, dance, etc. . . . . ! All we need is plenty of cheering and the only way to get that is for you to be there!

We have had a big job keeping the plans away from the football team; as far as we know, they don't know that any celebration is being planned. So, if you are going to Ripon on Saturday, or if you talk to any of the players by phone, please make sure they know nothing about the celebration.

Remember: EVERYONE BE OUT TO GREET THE TEAM. *If you have any ideas to make the celebration bigger and better tell your floor representatives. If you are called on to work Saturday, please respond.*

Above all . . . better . . . BE THERE TO:

1. *Welcome home the Midwest Conference Champions.*
2. *Welcome the team that has won more conference games in Midwest Conference history.*
3. *Welcome home one of the few undefeated and untied teams in the nation!*

It was about midnight on the following Saturday when the team bus approached the campus. It broke through a huge banner reading "WELCOME HOME, CHAMPS." The bus drove slowly around what was called the Bald Spot. Over eighty torches lit the way. The bus rolled up in front of Sayles Hill Gym and was greeted by a cheering student body. Each athlete had a lei put around his neck, had his picture taken, and heard a roar of appreciation as he stepped off the bus.

I found another memento in my files:

Just a note of appreciation for the wonderful experience of Saturday evening. To me, it was the finest demonstration in all my coaching years.

Please convey to your committee my sincere appreciation of their great efforts. I am mighty proud of being associated with Carleton and shall treasure this as one of my finest memories of this association.

Chet McGraw

Dean Kille was right—go for something creative. The celebration worked. Everybody remembered the event. A day of canceled classes, though fun, would have soon been forgotten.

A Year at Yale

After graduating from Carleton in June 1955, I went home to Omaha for a few days. At the end of the month I took a Greyhound bus to New Haven, Connecticut, arriving at 3 A.M. I spent my first night at the YMCA. The next day I joined Yale's Master of Arts in Teaching program, where I would take the education courses needed for certification to teach in public schools. I found four roommates, and we rented an apartment from a dentist whose offices were at 322 George Street.

As I had done at Carleton, I wrote letters home from Yale, and my mother saved them. The graduate courses, like education courses most everywhere, were pretty routine and unexceptional. But certain people and events stood out.

Magda

Long before my roommates and I arrived, the dentist had hired a cleaning lady named Magda. I wrote to my folks about her.

Magda is foreign born, must weigh two hundred pounds, and plods around in her bare feet. The other day I offered her a plum and she said: "Oh, no tank you. I canna eat no fruit." I asked her why. She replied, "Cussa da Lord don bless da fruit 'til August twenty-eight." She is sweet and has a rock hard faith.

The other day I came home and she said, "Shhh, donna you tell no one but I moppa you floor for you. Other day you helpa me openna da vindow, so today I moppa your floor. Shh, donna you tella doctor. He no lie me vorka for you when I shoulda be vorka for him."

And from another letter:

I may have lost a friend today. On this beautiful morning I headed out for class as Magda was sweeping the front walk. We exchanged a few words. Whatever the cue, perhaps she wiped the sweat off her brow, I, with all good humor, said, "Well, as they say, no rest for the wicked." What she said and what she did is a blur, but you'd have thought I'd threatened her with hell's fire and assured damnation. As I backed away apologetically, she simmered and steamed with anger.

Theater

For me, Yale's location in the East proved to be its greatest advantage. The area offered beaches, colonial-era towns and churches, opera in New York City, and especially theater—theater like I'd never seen in Nebraska or Minnesota. In the 1950s, many Broadway shows would have tryouts in New Haven before going on to New York.

In my year at Yale two shows stand out: a new musical by Rodgers and Hammerstein, and *My Fair Lady*. The Lerner and Loewe piece proved superior to the Rodgers and Hammerstein work. Their musicals lit up the American stage. I still hum many of their enchanting melodies from such hits as *South Pacific, Oklahoma!,* and *The Sound of Music.*

For more than fifty years this is what I remembered about the new Rodgers and Hammerstein show: I was sure it was called *Cannery Row.* Helen Traubel, opera's leading Wagnerian soprano, was making her debut in musical theater. The show was to open on a Monday night. The Saturday before, one of my roommates, Hank, and I decided to pose as reporters for the *Yale Daily News.* We walked from our apartment to the stage door of New Haven's Shubert Theater. Initially, our request to watch the rehearsal garnered a firm no, but we wheedled until the guard relented. "It's dark inside," he informed us, "but just edge around the stage curtain, go down the stairs, and sit in the seats."

We sat for several hours watching and listening as Rodgers and Hammerstein, the brightest lights in musical theater, rehearsed their new show. And we listened to Helen Traubel sing one of her solos.

That is how I remembered the event for many years. But among my Yale letters is one that gave a detailed account of what actually happened that afternoon.

DEAR PARENTS,

I'm glad to be writing when I'm fired up to tell you something. Don't get excited, I'm not married, but Hank and I did the greatest thing this afternoon from 3:30 until 6. The experience centers on the pre-Broadway Rodgers and Hammerstein musical "Pipe Dream" starring William Johnson and HELEN TRAUBEL. *We got the brilliant idea last night of going down to the Shubert Theatre and watching rehearsals. Since they were closed affairs, we explored ways to get in.*

I hit on the idea of posing as reporters from the Yale Daily News *and asking for an interview with a member of the cast. We could tell them that cast member "X" was a former Yale student and we wanted an interview. Sooooo, this afternoon Hank and I dressed up in our dark suits and off we went. I donned my horn-rimmed glasses and took my new briefcase, just to make things look official. We decided to walk in like we belonged, and only if we got caught would we use the reporter story.*

Incidentally, "Pipe Dream" will probably be the year's biggest musical. We found out that Rodgers and Hammerstein had bought all the stock in the play, which is a sign of their confidence. Though not opening on

Broadway until November, it's already sold out through the following April. They are opening in New Haven tomorrow night for a week to give the show a pre-Broadway trial.

We strolled into the lobby, past the box office, and into the darkened theater. I was tense. Our success was short-lived—the theater manager had seen us and came up seconds later. "Sorry, but rehearsals are closed to the public." He was cold and firm so we high-tailed it out. Hank suggested the stage door. I got a name of a lesser lead from the billboard, George Wallace. I figured we could use it. Hank insisted I do the talking.

At the stage door I asked for George Wallace. The guard didn't know much, but we told him we'd wait. Through the scenery I could see Miss Traubel on stage. I figured it would be enough if we could just stand there, but this too was short-lived. An authoritative-looking man came up and asked, "Whadda you want?" I said we were looking for a member of the cast, George Wallace. He told us to wait a minute. "I'll get him," he said.

We were tense. Hank pleaded, "Let's beat it." I stood firm. "Hell no, we don't have anything to lose." The guard shouted downstairs, "George Wallace." Next, William Johnson, the co-lead with Miss Traubel, appeared. "You lookin' for somebody?" I told him: "George Wallace." Johnson shouted around, and then, over the backstage microphone, we hear the announcement, "George Wallace wanted at stage door."

"What are we going to say?" Hank kept asking. I thought we would just tell the guy the truth. Soon Wallace appeared. "Someone looking for me?"

Asking him to step outside, I told him our story. Darn, he was a good Joe, and impressed by our determination. "Just a minute," he said. "I'll see." He disappeared, then came back. "Geez, no, I can't let you in this way. Rodgers and Hammerstein are both out front. They aren't even allowing friends of anyone in this afternoon. This is the first time the orchestra and cast have worked together, and we're opening tomorrow night."

We talked to him for a while about the show. "Oh, it's swell," he said. "Everyone in the cast likes it." He added, "Look, come on under the stage, and you can sit there and listen to the music right near the orchestra pit."

So in we went—down amid the cast, boxes, makeup, etc. We learned that the cast had been working with a piano for five weeks. Then he offered, "Listen, if you can go up those stairs over there, you'll be in the wings, then take a left. Go down the stairs into the theater and sit down. If you get caught, so what, you've gotten an interview." He chuckled.

We tried to look like we belonged, and headed up the stairs. In the wings, Richard Rodgers was talking to a group of the cast, but there was no turning back. Passing them, we went down into the darkened theater and sank into two aisle seats. I expected any minute to get tapped on the shoulder, but seconds ticked by and no tap. I motioned occasionally towards the stage so it would look like we were directors commenting on the scenery. We looked over and sitting about twelve seats away was Hammerstein. The cast was just finishing a ten minute break. "Okay, everyone on stage for the Cannery Row scene."

There we sat, faces down, tensing up every time someone walked by. The experience was tremendous. They ran through some chorus numbers, and sang several songs. The music is swell, typical Rodgers and Hammerstein. After about an hour, we wondered if we were going to hear Traubel, but it was terrific anyway to watch the composer and librettist going over their show—stopping to make little changes here and there. When one of them spoke, a member of the cast always answered, "Yes, Sir." Rodgers did most of the directing. Hammerstein just sat and commented to Rodgers.

Luck came when Rodgers shouted, "All right, will someone send for Miss Traubel." About ten minutes later the great lady appeared. She must weigh about 250 pounds but is charming and full of bounce. A real show-

man. I kept thinking that here is a singer whose voice was heard in opera houses all over the world. Her singing was beautiful—commanding and clear. You could tell she felt the music.

It was getting late so we decided to leave. As we left, Rodgers and Traubel and another lead were going through a song. Traubel kept saying to the orchestra, "May I just hear that part once more, the music is sooo beautiful, I want to roll it!!" Our friend Wallace came up and chatted for a while, asked us how we liked it, and told us about some of the other songs. I'd say two of the four we heard are going to be hits!

Hank and I decided that we were probably the first two people, not associated with theater, who had seen part of what may be a great musical! Hank and I are going to send this Wallace a telegram tomorrow night, wishing him good luck, and sign it, "The Two Yale Interviewers."

Love to you both, Bill

There is a postscript. I recently found out what happened to *Pipe Dream*. I learned that it ran for several hundred performances, then closed, and is considered as close to a flop as anything Rodgers and Hammerstein ever wrote. (*Pipe Dream*—not *Cannery Row*—appeared after *South Pacific* and before *The Sound of Music*.) In his autobiography, Richard Rodgers says the main reason the musical failed was their miscasting Helen Traubel in the role of Fiona.

Practice Teaching

My first foray into public school teaching came at New Haven High School. "Practice Teaching" was one of the courses required for certification and my master's degree. I recall only one incident. It took place in a geography class I taught for slow learners. In 1955–56, Africa was still divided among the colonial powers. One day the students were working at their desks on a map of Africa. The assignment must have been to name each country, including the European country that owned it. A student named Henry came up to my desk.

"Mr. Buffett, who owns the Belgian Congo?"

"Henry, who's buried in Grant's Tomb?"

"General Grant?"

"Right you are. Now, who owns the Belgian Congo?"

"General Grant?"

I wrote home about other incidents.

Friday, when I walked in with this other guy, the principal appeared and said, "One, two. You two will teach classes all day for teachers who are sick." My classes were Electronics, Printing, and Mechanical Drawing, not areas of my expertise. Guys in these classes are mostly goof-offs who want to take something easy. Fortunately, there were no discipline problems. When I think of some of the hell I had sometimes given school substitutes, I realized I was damn lucky!

Today we had a wonderful class. They were supposed to be working on Africa, but we got to discussing the American Negro in our democracy. Some did not want to give Negroes educational opportunities equal to whites if this meant they might assume power over whites. I stressed the incompatibility between equality of opportunity, basic to democracy, and being unwilling to give it to Negroes. We had a lively discussion. Enthusiasm is the best way to show that what you have is worth their knowing.

When practice teaching ended, students were asked to write an evaluation of our work. Included among my letters from Yale, written on lined paper, most in pencil, were twenty-nine letters of evaluation by some of my students. Here are a few of their comments.

He had a very good understanding of us. . . . There was one thing that seemed rather odd and that was his moving back and forth when he talks. Otherwise he presented himself fine with the class.

If you don't know an answer, he doesn't make you feel like a criminal. The students behaved very well with Mr. Buffett without his cracking a whip over their heads. I don't know what makes them act so.

Mr. Buffett had the ability necessary for being a good teacher, but somehow he did not get the respect normally given to a high school teacher. This was probably due to the fact that all his students knew he was inexperienced. His manner of presentation was good and he possessed an easy-going attitude which made him a favorite among us. I especially liked the way he treated all of us, not only as students but as friends.

If he got mad, he got mad in a nice way.

Mr. Buffett was the kind of guy you don't forget easily. He was always good for a laugh but made it clear when the joking should stop. He could hold a class the same way a good actor holds his audience.

He was aware of all the sly tricks students could pull on teachers. One day he commented: "You must think I'm dumb. I know what you're trying to pull." It just happened that we were stalling for time so that he wouldn't give us homework. . . . I have a jumpy stomach and when Mr. Buffett gave a speech, he would sway back and forth and jingle the coins in his pocket. It would get me dizzy so I couldn't watch him without getting a headache. Maybe he was nervous.

On class control he did poorly. He had no rules for order. One day we would get away with murder and the next we would get detention. . . .

Another fault was always walking while he spoke. If he stood in one place he swayed, and brought a nauseous feeling over me.

He could not control the class very well, but I have had student teachers who were a lot worse. . . . He walked back and forth too much and gestured with his hands too much. Sometimes he would relax too much and loll on the furniture such as the table and shelf next to the window.

I think he made himself too comfortable by sitting on a table or desk. He always came to school looking neat, but at the end of the day he looked different. . . . He didn't use words which we never heard of before.

Mr. Buffett had a good personal appearance. He had a habit of saying "See," and he shook the ring finger on his left hand quite fiercely.

Another memorable event from my year at Yale took place in New York City. I wrote my parents:

After an afternoon nap we went off on another interesting adventure—to the Heaven of Father Divine. This is a religious cult headed by a Negro, Father Divine, who proclaims himself to be God. The cult accepts most of Christianity except that they believe it was Father Divine who sent Christ to earth. I didn't learn a lot of their theology, but that wasn't the important thing. We went into this large dining room where the tables were set and where there were about 250 followers, waiting to be fed. The gathering was about 98% Negro. The religion emphasizes emotion, and as we entered the audience was singing hymns. A woman, dancing up in front, seemed to be in a trance. The only musical accompaniment was a saxophone and a tambourine. They treated us fine. All seats were taken but several men got up and gave us their places.

During the meal there was a recorded speech by Father Divine, interrupted occasionally by "Amen," "You're right, Dear Father," "So Glad" and "Praise Him." (*Father was speaking from Philadelphia. We learned that he couldn't come to New York because he's wanted for tax evasion.*)

After Father's sermon various members of the gathering rose to give little speeches. One lady told about how Father had cured her husband of cancer; others also affirmed his power and divinity. They introduced each of us. Food was passed, family style, by the diners themselves. If I'd taken one of everything I would have had:

MEAT:	*spare ribs, fried chicken, chicken dumplings, ham, pork chops, and several others I can't remember.*
VEGETABLES:	*peas, carrots, corn, green beans, okra, spinach, greens, macaroni, rice, potatoes, rutabaga, and lima beans.*
SALADS:	*jello, cottage cheese, tomatoes, and lettuce.*
DESSERT:	*chocolate, peach, vanilla, and strawberry ice cream, apple pie, banana pie, jello, prunes and peaches.*
DRINK:	*ice coffee, ice tea, and water.*

I have never had so much food before me at one time.

In June 1956 I graduated from Yale, but I've never thought of myself as a "Yalie." Maybe that's because most of my memorable moments occurred outside the classroom. In September I began an eleven-year stint teaching history at New Trier High School in Illinois.

bella nozzal's dolmas

The bad thing about this recipe is that it is very labor-intensive. The good thing is that it makes the best stuffed grape leaves you've ever tasted, even if you have a recipe passed down by your great grandmother who grew up in the old country. Guaranteed.

dolmas:

½ cup cracked wheat in water to cover

½ cup butter

3 bunches green onions, chopped

2 lbs. ground sirloin

1 bunch fresh parsley, chopped

2 bunches fresh cilantro, chopped

2 bunches fresh dill

4 large cloves garlic, chopped

1 tablespoon curry powder

1 tablespoon turmeric

salt and pepper to taste

2 jars (16 oz. each) grape leaves

½ cup olive oil

juice of 2 lemons

1 cup water

yogurt sauce:

1 cup plain yogurt

1 cup sour cream

1 tablespoon chopped fresh dill

½ teaspoon salt

tomato sauce:

¼ cup butter or olive oil

1 large yellow onion, chopped

½ teaspoon cayenne pepper

1 can (8 oz.) tomato sauce

pita bread (for serving)

1. To make the dolmas, place the cracked wheat in a small bowl with warm water to cover. Let stand for 30 minutes. In a medium frying pan, melt the butter and sauté the green onions.

2. In a large bowl combine the ground sirloin, sautéed green onions, parsley, cilantro, dill, garlic, curry powder, turmeric, salt, and pepper. Drain the cracked wheat and add to the meat mixture. Mix well.

3. Drain the grape leaves and unroll them so they lie flat. Working with one leaf at a time, shiny side down, place a tablespoon of the meat mixture in the center. Fold in the four sides so they overlap and place the dolma, seam side down, in a wide soup pot. Form the remaining dolmas and place them snugly in the pan, layering them if necessary.

4. Pour the olive oil evenly over the dolmas. Add the lemon juice and the water. Cover and place over medium heat. Simmer gently until filling is cooked, 45 minutes to an hour.

5. Meanwhile, make the yogurt sauce. Stir together the yogurt, sour cream, dill, and salt until smooth.

6. To make the tomato sauce, sauté the onion in the butter or olive oil over medium heat until translucent, about 5 minutes. Sprinkle in the cayenne pepper and cook about a minute, then pour in the tomato sauce. Simmer 5 to 10 minutes to blend flavors. Keep warm.

7. Transfer the cooked dolmas to a large serving platter. Pour the yogurt sauce evenly over them, then pour the hot tomato sauce evenly over the yogurt sauce. Serve with pita bread.

Serves 6 to 8 generously.

Noah's Middle Name

In 1959, Elias Rigopolous and I stood in the village square in Andritsina in southern Greece. We were virtual strangers. I didn't learn his name until later. He spoke no English and I spoke no Greek. He was a blacksmith and I was a student—at the American School of Classical Studies in Athens—having the best summer of my life.

The story of why I eventually named my son after this Greek blacksmith begins earlier that spring. Mike Greenebaum and I were both high school history teachers, and one day Mike asked if I'd be interested in enrolling in a summer school in Greece. We applied, were accepted, and on June 10 boarded a Cunard liner, the Q.S.S. *Arcadia,* in Montreal.

Six days later we landed at LeHavre. We took a train to Paris, stayed a day, and then flew to Rome. For a week our base was the Hotel Tirreno. We visited many sites, took a train to Ostia Antica, once Rome's seaport, saw a performance of Puccini's *Gianni Schicchi,* and visited Spoleto's "Festival of the Two Worlds," where we heard the soprano Eileen Farrell.

Our flight to Athens left on the afternoon of June 27, and that night we had dinner on the veranda of Loring Hall, the dormitory of the American School. There were about twenty in our group, not including our leader, Professor C. A. Robinson Jr. of Brown University. We learned that during the summer we'd make three trips: one through northern Greece, one through the Peloponnese—southern Greece—and one to the island of Crete. Each student would prepare talks about two of the sites visited and do research in the school library. My first assignment was an ancient healing spa, the Amphiarian at Oropos, and my second talk would be at the Temple of Zeus at Olympia.

While in the Peloponnese, we arrived one afternoon at Andritsina, a little town near Olympia where I'd give my talk. Neither paved nor gravel roads greeted us. But there were donkeys, children, houses, and shops around a square in the center of which were a large tree, a spring, and a trough. Animals drank, and people filled cans and clay jars at the spring. The scene felt lively yet simple. It was siesta time, so most people were resting behind shuttered windows and closed doors. We checked into our hotel.

I wrote many letters home to my folks that summer.

We got settled in our Class E hotel—one toilet with no seat, a shower built out over the hill that had a barrel of water and a can with which you doused yourself, no running water in the rooms and electricity only from 8 'til 12—after that: oil lamps.

Then we headed into the hills to the Temple of Apollo at Bassae, one of the best-preserved ancient temples and built on a beautiful site. A few yards up the hill was another of the many circular threshing floors we've seen. Three men were driving a team of horses around and around over the grain. Every so often they would stop, and with their forks, throw the stalks into the air to remove the chaff. Each horse wore a bell around its neck and the sound added to the setting.

Mike and two other guys decided that since the hotel was so primitive and the temple so fine, they'd spend the night there. Normally I would have too, but at the moment it didn't sound very appealing.

The rest of us climbed in the bus and headed back to Andritsina. We had about two hours until dinner so I took a walk on my own. Up a shaded street I found two blacksmith shops side by side, each with cow, goat, and sheep bells hanging out in front. One fellow jangled his bells from inside; the other came out to get my attention. I decided to reward the latter's extra effort, and after comparing rings bought three small bells for 15 cents each. We smiled, parted, and I walked back to the village square.

Mrs. Robinson also wanted to buy bells. I took her to the shop—she bought eight and I bought seven more. Back at the hotel some others in our group were interested so I took them to the same shop.

That evening I was standing in the square watching several fellows unload watermelon when my blacksmith friend came up. He motioned me over to a table at a nearby taverna where several of his friends were sitting. There was a plate with meat and potatoes on it and four forks. We each took one and dug in. Soon beer was brought. The two other fellows were teachers at the local school. One spoke a little English, the other, a little French. The English teacher told me that the blacksmith's name was Elias and that he usually had one beer, but because business had been so good he was having two.

When we'd finished the food on the plate, Elias sent out a boy who came back in about five minutes with something wrapped in a newspaper. Elias laid it on the table and unwrapped lamb meat, heart, liver, and some fatty tissue. He gave it to the waiter, who went inside to have it cooked. In the meantime Elias and the English-speaking fellow exchanged words; then the teacher turned to me and said, "Elias wants know you sleep his house tonight?" "Nei," I said, at first hesitant, "Nei, nei."

Elias and I shook hands and I thanked him. Soon the wife and son of one of the men and the son of the English-speaking fellow joined us. Eventually the meat came and quite a pile of it there was—all chopped up in bite-size pieces—greasy and dark, but smelling good. Now we had eight forks, the communal plate, and of course, more beer. They asked me how old I was. When I told them 26, one fellow didn't believe me, but I got out my passport and pointed to the date. I also showed them my picture of Fritz. The English-speaking fellow said, "Please give your brother from us our greetings." I wanted to tell you all that!

The party broke up, and Elias and I headed toward his home. There were no streetlights; the road was dark, the sky was clear, and there were millions of stars. We walked about a quarter of a mile and met Elias's wife Ereketi filling her clay jug at a spring. I knew about ten words in Greek, but we had a fine time. As we walked I pointed to the sky and said, "Kala, Kala" (good, good)—there were plenty of warm smiles as we tried to understand each other and usually failed. Very soon we came to their home on the second floor of a two-story building, one of about fifteen homes scattered on the side of a low mountain.

When we walked up the stairs I asked to see their home. It consisted of a living room with a table in the middle and two cot beds along two walls. Among the pictures on the walls were four showing scenes from America, including one of Mount Rushmore. In another room, when they turned on the light it disturbed Ereketi's elderly aunt, who had been asleep. The room contained a few chairs, a radio, and a fireplace. Off that room was a kitchen minus a refrigerator, though one cupboard might have been an icebox. A large can with a spigot stood over a basin that served as a sink. There was no stove, but I did see a kerosene lamp for cooking. As in the other rooms, one bare light bulb lit the space. There was also a clothes iron with a compartment for hot coals. A large brick oven and the toilet were in the next room. Near the toilet was a pail of water and a can: it was a "flush-it-yourself" type. The couple's big double bed was in the last room. After the tour we went out to an open veranda with a hard dirt floor. There were pots of flowers and herbs, all protected by a grape arbor. Big bunches hung down, but they were still green.

Ereketi brought out chairs for Elias and me, and then water. We'd been told that we shouldn't drink the water, but being a guest, I couldn't turn it down. They thought I'd like to bathe my feet, so Ereketi warmed water as Elias and I looked out on the beautiful night. He got up and picked a sprig of one of his herbs for each of us to smell. Every so often one of us would think of something that could be expressed by using sign language and a few simple words. I learned that he had two young daughters that weren't at home, but I couldn't understand where they were. I told him the towns we'd visited in Greece and that I'd come to Europe by boat. Soon the water was ready and I went into the kitchen, where a rectangular wooden tub with soap and a can of warm water waited. As I soaped my feet, Ereketi poured warm water over them. When I finished she got a clean towel for me.

Elias came in as I was looking at some kitchen utensils. He reached up and gave me a little copper pot used to brew Turkish coffee. He indicated that it was mine, a gift. I was touched. Then we went into one of the rooms, and out of a cupboard came a huge box of photographs. Ereketi's aunt joined us. She was a big woman, a bit bleary-eyed, and wearing black, the color women wear for the rest of their lives when their husbands die. The four of us stood around laughing as they pointed out pictures taken many years earlier. Elias disappeared into the bedroom and came back with a small framed picture of him and his wife. He put it in my hand. I indicated that it was too good to give away, so he found a snapshot of him and his wife that I still carry in my billfold.

He turned on the radio, and while we were listening to music, he walked over to the fireplace and took down two empty shell cases, each now holding a flower. Elias explained that they were from the Greek-Turkish war of 1918, in which his father had fought. I looked them over, and Elias pushed one toward me. I was to take this, too. I showed him that the pair was necessary to decorate each end of the shelf and said no several times, but it didn't work.

At around 11:30 they showed me my bed: THEIR big double bed. They insisted, saying that they would sleep in the beds in the living room.

Ereketi opened the windows in their room to the cool breeze. I looked out on the stars, the hills, and the town. I remember lying awake quite a while with tears in my eyes, thinking about their hospitality, the best I've ever known.

The first sound of the morning, "Bee-al," came from Elias at 5:30. Time to get up. He and I sat out on the veranda, overlooking the quiet town in the cool morning. It was light, but the sun hadn't yet climbed over the mountain.

Soon the procession began. It was Saturday, market day in Andritsina, and from the country to the town came farmers, donkeys, and horses laden with goods. Most people walked. The animals carried bags of wheat, loads of wood, and fresh vegetables; one bag had a little pig's head sticking out. Each animal had a bell around its neck. Imagine the sight and sound they all made. Ereketi brought two small cups of Turkish coffee and two glasses of water, the typical Greek breakfast. The young boy who worked in Elias's blacksmith shop arrived with a big can of water for the kitchen.

A woman passed in front of their house with a basket of fresh eggs on each arm. Elias sent the boy down to her, and in about fifteen minutes Ereketi brought out four warm, hard-boiled eggs and a dish of salt. Before I'd finished my first, she came with two more. She gestured that these were soft boiled. When we finished there were two eggs left. Ereketi gave them to me, wrapped in a piece of newspaper.

At around 7 A.M. I said goodbye to Ereketi, adding "Ef-kare-e-sto" (thank you) several times. Elias and I walked into town. At his shop, I took his picture. We then walked back to his house so I could get a picture of him with his wife. Back to town. The bus wasn't to leave for another thirty minutes, so Elias and I sat down at a taverna and ordered coffee. Two other members of the summer session joined us, and he ordered coffee for them. I don't need to tell you who paid.

We all sat and watched the colorful activity in the square. Fresh vegetables of all colors, pigs and chickens tied to a stake, and a fellow with two boxes of fresh fish made up part of the scene. On one side of the square stood a line of about ten donkeys with grain sacks on their backs waiting in front of the merchant's shop. At about 8:15 we headed for the bus, Elias carrying my knapsack. It was a warm goodbye. As the bus rolled past their home, I saw Ereketi on the porch. I waved and yelled "Adio" (goodbye).

Over the years, we exchanged letters that I had translated from English into Greek or from Greek into English. One letter contained a sprig of thyme from their patio. If anyone I knew was going to Greece, I'd tell them about Elias and Ereketi.

Nineteen years passed. I hadn't been in touch with my friends from Andritsina for a long time. In the interim I'd been married, had two children, and gotten divorced. By 1978 I'd met Susan, my future wife, and together we decided to go to Greece. We rented a car and drove through the Peloponnesus.

I kept a journal, and on Sunday, August 27, I wrote:

Yesterday we drove into Andritsina in mid-afternoon. I recognized the square and found the street on which Elias's blacksmith shop had been. We went to a small restaurant at the end of the street and made inquiries. People recognized Elias's name, but a boy who spoke some English wasn't sure whether he was there or in Athens. (As we ate we listened to the boy's grandfather and another man talking. Later I asked what they had been talking about, and he replied, "They were talking about religion. Everyone has a different opinion of whether there is a God or not.... It's a very difficult question.")

The boy, his younger brother, and a friend took us through Andritsina to Elias's house. As we approached I looked at several white houses on the hillside. I thought I knew Elias's, but I was wrong. The Rigopolouses lived next door to it, though, so we climbed the stairs.

The first words I heard were "Beel! Beel! Beel!" echoing in the air. Ereketi and I hugged. Soon Elias, roused from his siesta, showed up, sleepy-eyed, and there were more hugs. One of Ereketi's brothers appeared. He recalled how I had bumped my head on the door frame and imitated my long stride. Lemonade and Coke were served. I got out an old letter I'd received from them many years before which contained a dried sprig of thyme. When Ereketi saw it, she stood up and plucked a fresh sprig from the same plant.

Elias and Ereketi's daughters, Aloi and Yia, were now grown with children of their own. They helped interpret. They told me about a woman "from Beel" who had shown up one summer, and about the two men who had knocked on the door one winter night with meat and wine "from Beel." I didn't remember them. The children loved to yell "tourist" then duck behind a curtain.

Elias and I walked into town for more meat, and for dinner, besides the souvlaki, we had salad, feta, bread, fried potatoes, and beer. For dessert: watermelon. Susan and I had a bed to ourselves, the same one I'd slept in many years earlier.

The next morning, we had warm milk with sugar, along with Greek coffee, butter, bread, and honey. We left at about nine. Ereketi gave Susan a crocheted doily and two pillow cases made from home-spun cloth about fifty years before. She brought out a picture I'd sent of my parents and me. There were many tears when we left. As we drove off Elias stretched over some bushes to prolong the goodbye. His is the last face I saw.

By the following June, Susan and I were married and our baby boy was born. We named him Noah Elias Buffett-Kennedy. I sent a picture of him to Elias and Ereketi and said I'd named him after one of the finest men I'd ever met.

We had learned on our visit to Andritsina that Elias's health wasn't good, and one night a call came from Athens that he had died. I had the following note translated into Greek:

DEAR EREKETI,

I have thought of you and Elias, and of Aloi and Yia so often during these past months. I feel a deep sorrow because of the death of your husband and my friend, Elias. It saddens me to know that I shall not see him again, but I am grateful that we were together in the summer of 1979 and that our lives touched in such an unusual and wonderful way. I wish that I might have been with you before he died and that I might be with you now. I send you my deepest sympathy in what I know is a very sad time.

I told her a little about our family:

We are all well here in America. My parents, who live in Nebraska, are coming back to Massachusetts in May to visit us. My two older children, Wendy and Tom, are working hard in school and both had birthdays in March. Wendy is 17, Tom is 15. Noah Elias is a fine baby. He is very healthy and strong. He crawls very well and can pull himself up to tables and chairs. I took him to a beach yesterday and he ate his first mouthful of sand. Please do not think that feeding sand to babies is another strange American custom. It is just that he is quick and his father was looking the other way. Soon he will be able to walk. Susan and I love him very much. He is happy and doesn't cry often.

Eight years later, again on a summer afternoon, Susan and I drove into Andritsina. This time Noah was with us. We climbed the stairs. A radio played inside. Someone was at home. We knocked and Ereketi answered. As she embraced the boy named after her husband, tears flowed. Noah asked to see Elias's grave, so the four of us piled into our small car and drove down a rutted dirt road to a simple cemetery.

I came upon the grave of Elias Rigopolous by accident, like finding a rare gem on the path of one's life. Elias and Ereketi had welcomed me into their home, given me their bed, and fed me. Noah is now thirty and in law school. His last name combines my name and his mother's. His first recalls the Old Testament story of Noah and the ark.

I trust that our son will build upon the generous hospitality that is already a part of his character, a hospitality that echoes that of his other namesake, Elias. I hope his life is similarly enriched by the joy of a chance encounter.

harvard doctorate

silver lining

hacking license

queen victoria

square coffin   stained tie

scooped   highway robbery

hot pants   electric guitar

symphony hall

defense stamps

voucher   knuckles   life saver

howard johnson's   alaska street

dialysis machine   boston celtics

DOWN AND DIVORCED

toothy grin

lady of the laundry

green ottoman

king tut

gizzard

artificial leg

fake eyeball

love duet

suburban brick

thumbprint

old pops

maku

smart old shoe

mustard plant

heart afire

social insects

baby squirrels

brief beatitude

honeymoon

death valley

cambridge co-op

ever pitch

petunia

london bookstores

dog breeder

entangled bank

lincoln logs

hermaphrodites

leaf cutter

waist-high cases

craggy throne

muslim

strong right arm

ouster

laundry carts

fine-grained leather

cross-country skiing

new york subways

cardboard box

grain mill

nixon

prayers

pearl harbor

lak

law of gravity

conch shell

sultan muhammad

well-oiled door

Checker #74

It's difficult to explain why someone in his early forties with two graduate degrees, including a Harvard doctorate, opts to drive a cab. Sitting behind the wheel of a taxi was truly a last resort, a "don't know what else to do, the future feels closed" decision. Years later I learned that my parents weren't proud.

There is an adage: "Every cloud has a silver lining." No cloud in my life has had more of a silver lining than driving a taxi. I look back on the experience as one of the best in my life. At the time, however, I took small comfort when someone said, "You don't sound like a typical cabdriver."

Hacking gave me ample time to write letters to my folks and to my brother and sister-in-law. They saved the letters, and I have mined them for excerpts. Here's part of a letter I wrote to my folks in 1975:

Today I go in for my physical, get a hackney license, take a street test, and eventually work the 5:30 a.m. to 3:30 p.m. shift. I'm entering a different world, but will have a job and bring in some money, and I've already met a few characters.

Mr. Becker, who works in the employment office, is very short and very fat, and what the historian Barbara Tuchman said about Queen Victoria applies—when he goes it will be in a square coffin. He wore a mod, multicolored shirt, adorned with a stained tie, and over it all, like a limp, loose wrapping, a blue suit from the Salvation Army. Mr. Becker drove for Checker for twenty years, and told me, "We need you and you need us."

Harvard never said that.

Driving around Boston today, thirty years later, I still recall certain passengers. Right over there, at the corner of Massachusetts Avenue and Boylston Street, I picked up a lady going to her dental appointment. All the way, she talked about her teeth and nothing else.

Finally, I'm free to speak my mind. "For God's sake, lady, shut up. I'm not interested in your damn teeth. Save it for the dentist." But I listened politely, of course—tips counted, and they added up. I remember my first week's paycheck. I made $63, plus tips, for five ten-hour days. It wasn't much and, though better than nothing, wasn't as much as if I'd collected unemployment.

Do you know what being "scooped" means? Or "stiffed"? I didn't, until I drove a cab. One day someone from Cambridge phoned Checker and ordered a cab. I took the call and got the job, meaning that the dispatcher heard my number first when I pressed the button on my radio and yelled into the mike, "Cab 74, Cab 74." The dispatcher responded, "Cab 74, 3240 Mass. Ave. in Cambridge for Watson." As I approached 3240, I saw another cab, a Cambridge Checker, drive off with my fare. I'd been scooped.

During my first week on the job, I picked up a tipsy woman at the Massachusetts General Hospital who wanted to go to Cambridge Hospital, a five-dollar ride. When we arrived, she simply got out and walked away without paying. I'd been stiffed.

Another example of someone not paying: early one morning I answered a call for the Chandler Hotel on Warren Street. The place had a reputation for being used by prostitutes; that morning two fellows came out and climbed in. They didn't tell me where they wanted to go, but instead asked if I liked Chinese food. "Sure, " I said. So they directed me to Chinatown, where I waited while they disappeared into an all-night restaurant. I kept the meter on.

They soon came out with food for the three of us. As they ate, I drove them to their next stop, an Irish pub in South Boston. While they went in, I dug into my Chinese food. The meter was running.

Fifteen minutes later they came out and wanted me to drive them to another pub. Again, I waited for them in the cab, and I finished my Chinese food. The meter stayed on. Eventually they came out and gave me the address of another pub. By this time, the meter read over thirty dollars. When I mentioned their paying, one said, "Hey, we bought you the food," in a "How could you?" tone. They didn't actually refuse to pay, but when we stopped at the next tavern I called the garage and asked for the police.

When the cop came, I told him I'd been driving these guys to pubs, they'd run up a thirty-dollar meter, and they now refused to pay. My fantasy was that he would unsheath his pistol, march into the place, and demand the thirty bucks. It didn't happen. The cop told me simply, "Take it up with Checker." Clearly what I considered highway robbery was, to him, a "kitten in a tree" call.

I pulled away and later told my story to Tom Murphy, a Checker traffic manager. The Chandler had an account with our company, and a week later I received a check for the unpaid fare. I wasn't stiffed, but I could have been. And no tip.

Cab 74. For more than a year it was a big part of my identity. Later, 74 became my lucky number. Our zip code is 02474, our phone number is 648-7421, and the address of the hospital where I eventually got a job was 74 Fenwood Road. I never became a cab driver's cab driver—someone who's driven for years, has a thousand stories, and knows every back alley in Boston—but I did good work.

Learning the business took a while. New to the city, I asked my peers, "How do I know how to get to where someone is going?" One driver said, "Most passengers know the best way to go." He was right. They did. But a Boston street directory and a map were always by my side.

On one cold winter morning, my first passenger—clearly a lady of the night—climbed in at the Lenox Hotel. She wanted to go home, to Mattapan, and knew the way. "Oooh, it's cold, it's so fuckin' cold," she said. "Enough of these hot pants and hose; I'm gonna get me some regular pants, a sweater, scarf, stocking hat, and gloves." When I suggested her business would plummet if she dressed like that, she shot back: "It couldn't get much worse than it is now, not for me, honey." In the midst of our talk she interrupted: "Oh, I don't feel good about this. You're not police, are you?"

I took her home to River Street in Mattapan, to her husband and two children, a boy and a girl, ages one and three. "I love 'em to death," she told me. As I watched her head for her front door, I realized that she and I had a lot in common. We both adored our two kids; we both had a sense of humor, and we both had atypical occupations.

I remember a young African-American driver I met one day in the taxi line, or "pool," at Logan Airport. Whenever our paths crossed, we had good talks. I saw him for the last time at the Dunkin' Donuts on Boylston Street across from the Lenox Hotel. Every morning after leaving the garage at 5:30 A.M. I'd go there to buy a paper, get coffee and a doughnut, light up, and wait in line for a fare from the Lenox. I'd never seen my friend there and hadn't seen him in several months. But he appeared that morning. He greeted me with a "Hi, teach!" and I said, "Hi, guitar player." After a brief chat he told me I wouldn't be seeing him again. He was buying an electric guitar and leaving for California. He reached over, shook my hand, and said, "Have a good life."

My funniest memory came from another driver. Estelle, one of Checker's longtime employees, wore thick glasses and smoked non-stop. Her sweaters were pockmarked with little burn holes. One day a fellow got in her cab at Logan and asked for the cheapest whorehouse in town. Estelle turned and said, "Honey, you're in it."

Not so funny was the Monday morning I reported for work and got called on the carpet. The prior night, the company's owner had driven down St. Botolph Street, where I lived, not far from the Checker garage, and seen my cab parked at the curb. I confessed. The night shift was slow and I was tired. I'd parked and gone to sleep in my apartment. The owner didn't appreciate his capital sitting idle.

I'm still embarrassed about the time I picked up a nicely dressed lady on Beacon Hill. She asked to go to Symphony Hall, where she was to attend a meeting to select a new person to write program notes for the Boston Symphony Orchestra. Seizing the moment, I told her about my background in music and expressed interest in the job. Out of kindness, I think, she took my name and phone number. I wince every time I imagine her telling friends about her presumptuous cab driver.

One Sunday I answered a call for Angell Memorial, a veterinary hospital. A young couple and their dog climbed in the back seat. Soon a terrible smell wafted through the cab. "Don't worry," the fellow said, "our dog is on medication and upset. I'll clean it up when we get home." We arrived, they got out, and I looked back. Sure enough, a small brown puddle rested on the seat. The man came out and wiped it up. As I drove away, the smell cleared, and the next passenger never knew.

Another time, I picked up an older woman at the corner of Washington and Court who had been a nurse during World War II. I asked her a question no one else had been able to answer. In the 1940s, I told her, my Omaha grade school classmates and I were part of the war effort. Besides buying defense stamps and collecting newspaper, we learned to knit six-by-six-inch multicolored squares that were eventually sewn into blankets for the boys overseas. I never saw mention of these blankets in any book about the home front and never saw them in any exhibits of war memorabilia. I thought that along with bombs, planes, and tanks, blankets knit by little hands all over the country would make a great story—yet I'd never seen a word about them. But my passenger remembered those blankets well. She'd seen them and used them. She put to rest an unsolved part of my past. In the storehouse of my memory, I moved something from lost to found.

A recurring problem for cab drivers is locating a toilet. You can't open your trunk and find a men's room. You learn where they are. Some lavatories exceed every criterion, but you have to edge through fancy lobbies and walk down carpeted stairs, for example, at the Hotel Statler. Other places are okay, but parking isn't easy—for example, the Parker House and the Sheraton. A few, like the pool at Logan, stink and provide no paper. Others are fine, but cost a dime—true at the Lenox Hotel and the Greyhound bus station. One time I was driving by the telephone building when nature called. I parked but saw a fellow guarding the door. Maybe he would have let me pass, but just in case I told him I worked for the phone company and had a grant to record graffiti on the walls of company men's rooms. It worked.

I'd just returned from Logan empty and gotten in line at Massachusetts General Hospital when Murphy, a black driver of Cab #30, pulled up behind me. He soon appeared at my window.

"Hey," he asked. "Do you have a dry pocket?"

"A dry pocket?"

"Yeah, I wanna piss."

We laughed as he headed for a toilet in the General.

I often think of an older couple I picked up at Mass General. Clearly, he'd just been discharged, and his wife was helping him get home. During our conversation, he said some words I've never forgotten: "Yes, as long as you can get up in the morning and put on your own clothes, you have a lot going for you."

I remember another man, Philip Baker, who lived in the Charlestown housing projects with his wife. Both were blind. He went once a week to Mass General to fold bandages in the Patient Activities Room. I asked if he would please ask for Cab 74 when he called Checker to order a taxi. He did.

He told me that as a young man he'd come to America with his older brother from Vilna, Poland. His folks were already in this country, where his dad worked as "a poor tailor making $13 to $14 a week." When I met Philip, he knew he'd been born on March 15 but didn't know his age; he thought he was "65, 66, or 67? Somewhere in there." He'd come to this country aboard the *Mauritania* as a teenager. Though he had brought identity documents with him, he said, "I threw 'em all overboard. Vat I need deese for?" He told me that he and his brother had originally left Vilna for Hamburg and from there traveled "in a little boat like a canoe it was" to Liverpool. They went to a cheap hotel and that night went for a walk. Seeing a sign that was half in Hebrew and half in English, they knew it was a house of God.

"We walked in and a young lady came over. 'Shalom,' she said, and took us to a big room with a cross and Star of David where men and women were reading the Bible. I started talking to her and she told me it was called Missionary House for Jews and non-Jews. When I told her I was going to Boston, she told me that she had a sister there, and added that someday she and I would meet again. 'Yes,' I replied, 'if God is good.'"

In Boston, Philip went to a school for foreigners and got a job at seven dollars a week tying newspapers. One night, two years after he arrived, he walked down Joy Street, across Beacon, and into the Boston Common. "I hear a young woman's voice, 'Gasp-a-din refoal,' and I reply, 'Raspitee borishna'—Good evening, young lady. The young woman from Liverpool had appeared! We talked, and I took her to a drug store on Washington Street for a soda. You know, six weeks later, I married that girl. She died in 1945. Her name was Rebecca. We were very happy."

I always asked Philip to sit in the front seat so we could talk. One day he advised me, "Try to do something, and do something good, but not too good. People will take advantage of you." In another conversation, he told me that his second wife was beautiful. When I asked him how he knew, he replied, "People tell me." And when I asked him how marriage was, he replied, "Well, ya gotta overlook a lot."

I remember the parting scene once we'd arrive at Mass General. A voucher provided him a free ride, but when I came around to help him out, he would stand by the door, take my hand in his, and press a quarter into my palm, saying, "May the sunshine follow you and you turn this quarter into a hundred dollars." I'd then take him into the Patient Activities Room. He didn't like the job, though, because it didn't pay anything. He complained, "I been comin' here eleven years, not a penny. I mik connin balls, sort bottles, mik bandages. All dey giff is a cup a coffee ant a coupla cookies. Huh! Beeg deal!"

I once picked up a man with a bandaged hand at Mass General. He worked nights in Park Square at the Pussy Cat Lounge, where they have both billiards and a bar. At closing time the previous night, he told me, a couple of pool players wouldn't leave, and a mini-brawl broke out. Later that night, while counting the cash, he felt pain in his hand, which had turned red. He got a ride to the General, where they found a piece of a tooth embedded next to one of his knuckles.

Cab drivers try for steady customers—people who travel regularly and agree to ask for your cab. I had a couple besides Philip Baker. I regularly took a lady from the Jamaicaway Hospital to Dana Farber for cancer treatments, and I took a woman named Mrs. Homsey, whose son owned an Italian restaurant downtown, for a weekly lunch of scallops. Every time she rode she asked me, "Would you like a Life Saver?"

Mrs. Homsey was in her mid-eighties, I'd guess, and had 90 percent of her marbles. She always sat in front, and we'd often stop at a drug store to get some "medicine," her Life Savers. She always traveled with a nice woman who took care of her. On her first trip, I rang the bell and waited about eight minutes for Mrs. Homsey to come down and get in the cab. The aide whispered to me, "Look, after this, just turn on the meter when you ring the bell. She can afford it, believe me."

So the next Wednesday I rang the bell, returned to my cab, turned on the meter, and started to read the paper. After a while, Mrs. Homsey toddled out followed by an aide I'd never seen before. She looked only a little more stable than Mrs. Homsey and none too pleasant.

We started off, and I didn't bother to ask them where they were going. We went about a third of a block when the two of them began to argue about their destination. I stopped until they finally agreed to go to the Howard Johnson's on Commonwealth Avenue. Swear words went through my mind. The place was about a block away. We pulled up. I turned off the meter and went around to help Mrs. Homsey.

"How much?" asked the aide.

I looked at the meter and said, "A dollar thirty."

"A dollar thirty?" the aide said. "Last week we came over here for seventy cents!"

"Well, the meter reads a dollar thirty."

"Oh, no, it can't be. Something's wrong. Last week we came over here for seventy cents."

"Well, have you heard about the new cab rates? Some cabs have them; some don't." (This was true, but I didn't tell her that mine was one that didn't. And I didn't tell her that I had been instructed by the other aide, the nice one, to start the meter when I arrived.)

"Well, we came over here last week for seventy cents."

I could tell by her look that she was a mean one, but sometimes things like this work in your favor. We were parked in a single-lane drive, and several cars behind me were waiting to drive through.

Mrs. Homsey, now out of the cab, was searching for money. She had the dollar but couldn't come up with thirty cents. As she fumbled through several coin purses and the pockets of her coat, the cars behind me started honking. The aide opened her own purse; then Mrs. Homsey found the thirty cents.

Fortunately, the aide had Mrs. Homsey to take care of and heard the horns—enough to make her forget that they had gone there the previous week for seventy cents.

I picked up a very special woman one Friday at 9 Alaska Street in Roxbury. Mrs. Marshall was on the far side of middle age, plainly dressed, and black. She wore thick glasses. She sat in the front seat and asked to go to Mass General, where her husband was a patient. Several times she expressed the fear that they were "spearamentin' on 'im."

Five years earlier he had contracted kidney disease, she told me, and had to go on dialysis. In June, he'd had a transplant. Everything had gone fine until the previous Thursday. He'd gone to the clinic for a check-up and they'd found he had a temperature of 104°, the first sign that the body was beginning to reject the new kidney. Mrs. Marshall told me that when he got the news tears came to his eyes.

"You know what it means to be on a dialysis machine year after year," she said, "three times a week, needles and needles, blood flowing through tubes. Then comes the transplant and soaring hopes, the possibility of freedom from the machine. Then on Thursday, the sad news and the tears."

She was a soft-spoken, religious woman. She knew how hard it is to think of losing a loved one, but was convinced that "God knows what is best." At one point, I asked her: "Tell me, what is the third letter of your first name?"

"Well, let's see"—now counting on her fingers—"it's an 'R.' Why?"

"Well, the way it's written on the slip, I can't tell if it's 'Laneda' or 'Lareda.' I've never heard either name before."

"It is rare. I've never met anyone named Lareda either. 'Cept last year my cousin was blessed with a baby girl, and they named her Lareda. I looked up my name once and found it means 'Victory.'"

"My name's William and it means 'Courage.'"

"My, oh, my, isn't that nice. 'Courage.' Oh, that's good, that is."

"Well, there's often a difference between what a person's name means and what they are."

"Oh, I know I'm what my name means. Yes, I do. I'm 'Victory.'"

She turned, looked at me, and beamed. At that moment, she saw me as courageous. If she'd given voice to her thoughts, she might have said, "Oh, you're courageous all right. I can see that. Yes, sir."

But I couldn't bask in her light. I didn't feel at all courageous.

My short times with Lareda were like watching a sunset or listening to a symphony. One day she told me she'd gotten a little dog called Dusty and went on to say that she was taking her husband his breakfast: sausage, eggs, and grits.

"He won't eat hospital food. I'm also takin' him a six-pack of Coca-Cola. This way it's cheaper. At the hospital it's thirty cents a shot. If he don't pull out of it this time, he's goin' straight to hell." She said this with no meanness, but very matter-of-factly.

"Why?" I asked.

"He's ornery. He goes to church even when I don't go sometimes; but he say and do things that hurt people. Some people just have a nasty disposition.

"But I'm getting my reward. I get everything I need. Yesterday I came home from the hospital, and was too tired to go shopping. I'm sittin' there worryin', and there's a knock on my door. It's my daughter from Framingham. She goes out and gets me some food. Then she goes through my purse and says, 'Why, you only have three dollars. Tomorrow I'll bring you ten dollars.' You see, I'm getting my reward."

Driving a cab was okay at times, but it sure made me tense—the traffic, the exhaust fumes, waiting in line for a fare. The people's stories made it more bearable. One afternoon I tracked my rides over a few hours: a piano student at the New England Conservatory, a secretary who worked for the Boston Celtics, and a counselor who worked with disturbed children at a nearby state hospital. He told me that the courts sent children there. Among those he counseled was a six-year-old boy who had killed his four-year-old sister.

One day I stopped at McDonald's and bought a hamburger and carton of milk to have in my cab as I waited in line at the Statler. I took the paper off the hamburger and opened the carton of milk. I put the hamburger between my teeth and the milk on the dashboard.

The taxi line moved up and so did I—too abruptly. The milk tipped onto the steering column, glanced off my right knee, hit the seat, and sloshed onto the floor. I took a napkin and wiped off my maps, a book, my waybill, and five or six other things that had been hit. I cleaned off the dashboard. I took an old rag and ground it with my foot into the dirty-white pool that rolled around on the floor. It was a hot day and even with the windows open my cab smelled sour. I had to drive home to change my pants.

My next fare, a businessman at the Colonnade Hotel, told me where he wanted to go, leaned forward, and asked, "What is that strange smell?"

"Oh, don't worry," I said, still upset about spilling my milk and all the time I'd lost having to go home and change. I didn't want to tell him, so I said my last fare was a young mother with a tiny baby who had spit up. I could imagine the guy looking nervously at the seat, but my comment worked. It shut him up. I was in no mood to talk.

The second day I went in to Checker—I was still in the process of applying for the job—a kid drove in, somewhat dazed. It was his first day driving; in fact, he'd just left the garage. He'd been robbed and hit in the face by two fellows he'd picked up in front of Northeastern University, about three blocks from the garage.

A leader in the Teamsters local, to which drivers must belong, spoke to me and two others one day after work. "You get robbed, beat up, and you're lying in the hospital. You think anyone around here gives a damn? Ha! You're all alone. That city out there is a fuckin' jungle."

I talked to a nice young black guy one day while waiting in the pool at the airport.

"Are there any fares you don't pick up?" I asked.

"Yeah, young blacks, males, especially if there are two or more."

I was driving down Columbia Road early one Sunday afternoon, paying half attention to some talk over the radio about Cab #109. Pretty soon I saw a fire engine and Cab #109 parked at a corner. A fireman was in the cab. I stopped and got out. He told me the driver had been robbed and hit over the head. "Nothin' serious," the fireman added.

I waited for the ambulance and followed it to City Hospital. Incredibly, on the way it stopped to pick up the victim of an auto accident. At the hospital, they put the cabbie in a wheelchair and bandaged his bloody head. I got a couple of phone numbers from him—his roommates and his parents—so I could tell them what had happened.

One time I did a temporary assignment as the day driver of Cab #9. On the second day, the assigned night driver returned after three weeks in the hospital. He told me that one night he'd answered a radio call to an apartment building. When he rang the bell, a young black couple was waiting with a gun. They demanded his money. He turned and ran and got shot in the back. I asked him how he was feeling.

"Pretty good," he said, " but my bowels don't work right."

The traffic manager of Checker wrote a letter to the Boston Police Department asking for more protection for cab drivers. The letter listed specific dates when cab drivers were robbed and assaulted near the Bromley-Heath public housing project. It ended by calling the area dangerous and asking for help.

A few days later, a driver for Town Taxi, another cab company, was robbed and shot to death in the Bromley-Heath project. About a week later a special procedure was set up. If a driver picked up a fare that looked suspicious or if the fare was going into a high-crime area, he radioed in. For example, "Code 900, Cab #74 going from the Brigham Hospital to Bromley-Heath. Expect to arrive in about ten minutes."

The dispatcher then called the police, who were supposed to be there when the cab arrived. I never used Code 900. It can't happen to me, I thought, and in the eight weeks the procedure had been in operation, not one cab driver had been robbed in the Bromley-Heath area.

One Sunday I cruised by the taxi stand at Brigham Hospital. There were no Checkers so I pulled over and got out the *Times* crossword puzzle. I'd sat for ten minutes when two young black males asked if I was free. Both were around twenty, of medium build, and neatly dressed. They got in and asked to go to Wensley Street. I'd never heard of it, but one said, "It's just ahead, down Tremont."

"Do you go to church?" one of them asked.

"Well, I used to, but not much anymore. Why?"

"Oh, man, I was just wonderin', man, 'cause I went this mornin' for the first time. Down at St. John's, ya know, man."

"What denomination is that, Episcopal or what?"

"It's Baptist, ya know."

"How'd you like it?"

"Oh, man, it was pretty good, ya know."

"Turn here on Parker." It was the other guy speaking for the first time. "Just straight over the hill. Now down here take a sharp right."

I looked up and saw the street signs: Parker one way, Wensley the other. We turned right and headed up Wensley. There were a few rundown houses on both sides. Some kids had taken the cap off a hydrant and were playing in the water. I drove to an embankment on the left that sloped toward the projects; to the right were vacant lots. I didn't get suspicious but thought it odd that someone would want to be dropped off in such a deserted area.

"Just pull up in front of that blue truck," the second guy said.

"Here?"

"Yeah, that's okay. We can walk the rest. What does the meter say?"

"A buck twenty."

The second guy said to the first, "I'll give you fifty cents when we get up to the house."

I was waiting for the first to hand the money through the hole in the plastic partition. Suddenly the second guy appeared at my open window. I looked up to see him holding a small silver-plated pistol.

"Okay," he yelled in an angry, demanding voice, "we want your money." He pushed the pistol against my head just above the ear. "I oughta kill you, 'cause you're a white motherfucker."

By this time the first guy was at the window. He reached into my shirt pocket—a favorite place for drivers to stash their money. "Come on, come on, where is it?" I don't clearly remember the rest. It happened fast. One of them cleaned out my billfold and my briefcase. The other held the gun and ripped the mike off my radio. About thirty seconds later they backed away from the cab. One of them aimed the pistol at me and yelled, "Okay, you motherfucker, I'll give you five to get out of here. Then I'll blast your head off."

By one and a half, I'd left.

I went back to the garage and talked briefly with the traffic manager, then went to the District Two Police Headquarters to report the robbery. The man took down the details I remembered. I looked through three books of mug shots but didn't recognize anyone. I remember the cop saying, "Ah, Wensley Street. It's a favorite for these guys; they just run down the hill and disappear into the projects."

On my way from the police station to the garage, I went back up Wensley Street—the kids were still playing near the hydrant—and came to Heath Street. My "friends" weren't around. I had no idea what I would have done if they had been.

Back at the garage, I filled out another report, an Offense Against Checker form, and a Radio form indicating that my mike had been stolen. The most striking thing about the whole event was how routine my getting robbed at gunpoint was to Checker and to the police.

One of my most memorable fares came from Dorchester on a welfare voucher and needed to go to Mass General. Edward, a young man with scraggly black hair and brown skin, came out five minutes after I rang the bell, walking very slowly with a cane. His left arm dangled loosely at his side. He spoke in a quiet, calm voice, and asked to sit in front.

Right away he sounded like a good man. I wondered what had happened and why he was headed for a hospital. We talked for the next twenty minutes.

Early one morning a year earlier, Edward told me, he had been sitting in an office of the Suffolk County Courthouse, talking with another fellow also waiting for a clerk to open for business. Edward had gone to the desk to get a form and was sitting back down when a bomb went off. The fellow he'd been talking to suffered multiple fractures in an arm and a leg. "I lost my left leg," he told me. "My right leg doesn't work too well, and my left arm broke in three places. I'll never be able to bend it."

He'd been working in a hospital laboratory and going to school at night when his life crashed. He'd come to the United States from Trinidad four years ago "to find a better life."

In one letter to my brother and sister-in-law, I listed all thirty fares I'd had in one day; my comments told who they were, where I'd picked them up, and where I'd taken them. My eighteenth fare of the day had been the most interesting.

A nicely dressed, sixty-six-year-old black man, a gregarious, gentle, good-humored individual. I took him home after he'd been on a grand jury for a month. Two years ago, within the space of five months, he'd had four operations for cancer.

I asked him, "At sixty-six, what gives you happiness?"

He replied right away, "Jez bein' here. Jez bein' here. I find I got more time now to be nice to people; I'm kind to dogs; heck, I don't even mind the roaches so much anymore."

Driving a taxi wasn't all about fares, tips, waiting, and hustling. There was also life behind the scenes, at the garage. The two drivers of the same cab typically got to know each other. Both try to keep the cab clean and will often meet in the afternoon, when the day driver brings the cab in and the night driver is waiting to take it out. The night driver for Checker #74 was a bawdy young woman named Rose. She wanted to go to bed with me and let everybody know it. One of the drivers, Snooky, even asked me, "Hey buddy, when you gonna fuck Rose?"

I'd usually find Rose sitting by the trash heap as I came off the gas line in the afternoon. She'd climb in the front seat and we'd drive through the basement and up the ramp to ground level. A tunnel of love it wasn't. I had noticed that her greetings were becoming more than perfunctory. Occasionally she'd leave a note propped up on the ashtray. A couple of times she called my apartment.

One morning she called Checker and asked Cab #74 to take her home. Rose was white and about twenty-seven years old. She lived in Quincy with her boyfriend, who drove for another cab company. The dispatcher radioed me to pick Rose up at 1 Center Plaza. This lifted my spirits, but only because Quincy, well south of Boston, was a good fare.

Rose told me that she'd gotten into an argument with the driver of another cab. She tried to settle it by climbing on his hood and putting her heel through his windshield. When the glass shattered, the guy got scared and called the police. They came, arrested Rose, and put her in the Women's House of Detention in Pemberton Square for the night.

Breaking the guy's windshield and spending the night in jail still hadn't sapped her energy. In front of her house, she rumbled, "Ohhh, grrrr! I feel like wrestling somebody. Do you want to come in and wrestle?"

One good thing about Rose was that she obsessed about having clean windows and always carried a bottle of Windex. A bad thing was that guys liked to tease her by reaching under the hood and disconnecting her horn. Some mornings I'd get into Cab #74 to find clean windows but no horn.

Sadly, Rose sent no quiver through my loins. I fantasized sitting with her in a dark corner of the Checker garage, taking her hand, and saying, "I like you, Rose, but it wouldn't work. We come from different backgrounds. You're night shift. I'm day shift. We wouldn't stand a chance."

Long after I'd left cab driving, my second wife and I attended a church in the Back Bay area of Boston where, one summer, I was asked to give a Sunday sermon. I titled it "Images of Hope" and talked about three people who had given me hope. One was Amelia Gomez. This is what I said about her.

Amelia, a 67-year-old woman of Jamaican descent, lives on Rosseter Street in Dorchester, with a son, daughter-in-law, and two grandchildren. I haven't seen her in years and am certain I won't see her again. I met Amelia when I drove for Checker. The company had a contract with Mass General to take welfare patients to and from the hospital and I was one of the drivers who did the work. Amelia was one of the patients.

It was a chilly day in late November. The pick-up time was 9 a.m. and soon after I rang the bell, out she came. She walked slowly with two canes; one leg was artificial. I could see that the other was bandaged around the calf. She wore glasses, a wig, and a bundle of warm clothes.

"Give a poor old lady your strong right arm for a moment?" she asked, needing help down the steps. Her manner was direct and assured. Her "Give a poor old lady" was laced with twinkling self-mockery and said without self-pity. And when she said, "your strong right arm," my arm felt stronger than it had a moment before. We navigated the stairs and, when we got to the cab, she sat in the front seat. I reached down, and hoisted the fake leg off the street and into the cab.

The next thirty minutes, during our ride to the hospital, were an intense and memorable time. I'm tempted to ask, "What quality of Amelia Gomez's do you think I'll remember until the end of my days?"

Physically, she wasn't in top shape. Was it her forbearance in the face of physical adversity? That was there. Mentally she was sharp, made jokes, alas, even poked fun at me. Was it her good cheer and alertness? All that was there too. And I learned on a later trip that she read the Bible regularly. She had a special grace, no doubt, and faith, but it wasn't courage, alertness, good cheer, or faith that I remember first about Amelia. I wish, as I utter the word, for the presence of violins and ripe fruit, to better convey what was so special about her. What stood out was her sensuality. Amelia Gomez remains one of the most sensual people I've ever met.

Amelia talked of the convent school she'd gone to in Jamaica but not about the nuns or her classmates or her courses. She spoke with feeling of the boys lined up at the fence to see the girls march by on their way to class, how in the spring, there were even more boys and they were even more eager, because in the spring the girls wore short dresses and offered more for the boys to see and admire.

She told me how, when she was sixteen, one of those boys came to her one day, looked her right in the eyes, and said, "I want you."

And you could tell by the way Amelia imitated his "I want you" that she could not but acquiesce. At the time the boy, whose name was Robert, was twenty-five and Amelia was sixteen. "I tell him he have to wait two more years, until I eighteen."

He did and they were married.

"Oh, my mother objected," Amelia went on, "she wanted me to marry a white man like my sister did. And Robert was very, very black."

I asked her, "Who had the better marriage, you or your sister?" "Ah," she laughed, "I did by very much."

Then she told me that in their church the whites sat on one side and the colored on the other. Her sister and brother-in-law were divided.

"But Robert and I were together, and in church, I like to sit next to my man. I like to rub my leg against his. I like to take his arm and play with him, you know." Some time during that revelation her arm touched mine several times and I know I gripped the wheel tighter, and on that chilly day, my blood warmed.

As we drove down Charles Street, she told me how Robert would come home at night and say, "'Where is my midget? I want my midget.' And I would be in another room, maybe up on a ladder, cleaning or something, *and I would say, 'Who is that? What do you want? I beg your pardon sir, this is my house.' I tease him, you see."*

She mentioned having had five children, and as we pulled up to the hospital she added, "It was so nice when the last one left home. We felt much freer then."

I remained high that day from my encounter with Amelia. When my shift ended, I met a group of other drivers standing around in the garage. I told them about having met one of the most sensuous women ever and that she walked with two canes, had an artificial leg, and was sixty-seven years old. One of them looked up and said quite evenly, "Boy, are you sick!"

Once I picked up some tourists from the Soviet Union at the Statler and took them to the Museum of Fine Arts. We talked about opera and art, and they invited me to have coffee and a chat that night at the Statler. I was excited. I went from the museum to the Children's Hospital stand, and a doctor got in wanting to go to Brookline. In a rather ebullient mood, I asked him if anything exciting had happened that day. "No," he said. "Well, by golly, something unusual just happened to me," I said, and I told him about the Russians and our plans to meet again that night. I caught his toothy grin in my rearview mirror.

"Oh," he said, "they want to talk to the common American working man."

By Jesus, I almost went out of my mind. I wanted to take the ballpoint from its hole in the dashboard and do surgery on his bowel; instead I adopted a pensive tone. "Well, I really don't know," I said. "We talked mainly about the Bolshoi Opera, which I saw last year in New York, and about an exhibit of Russian masterpieces I'd seen several months ago at the Kubler Gallery in New York. We talked, too, about various Russian singers, composers, and paintings." I ended by saying I thought our "common" interests had led to the invitation. I thought to myself, Buster, you can call me "Bill" or any other name in the book, but don't you ever call me "common."

One fall day I was dispatched to the Don Orione Nursing Home for one "Blockel." I'd never been there before, but I knew it sat on a hill, an imposing complex of old brick buildings that provided nursing care and assisted living.

When I arrived, the front entrance wasn't apparent, so I stopped at the rear of a lone building. I got out of my cab near an open entrance. Light came into the hallway from a single open door. I walked in. Several big dryers and washing machines took up wall space, and in the center of the room were two large surfaces with ironing devices attached. A few laundry carts stood around, as well as three black-haired laundresses in drab gray uniforms. When I asked directions to the front entrance, they returned only polite smiles. English wasn't even their second language.

Suddenly, a head popped up from behind an overturned laundry cart, and an elderly nun gave me a suspicious look as if to say, "Who invades our space?" In broken English, and with a few gestures, she directed me to the front entrance. But before I could leave, she beckoned to me to approach. Pointing to the wheels of the laundry cart and holding up her old, arthritic hands, she showed me what she'd been trying to do. Each immobilized wheel was held firm by layers of tightly wound bits of thread. Not one wheel turned. While a few threads would be no problem, a compacted mass presented an impossible task for feeble fingers. She looked at me and back to the wheels, her intent clear.

I bent to the task. It wasn't difficult, but it took time. I hoped Blockel would still be waiting. Finally, with the axles bare, each wheel could spin freely. The nun beamed with gratitude. She stepped back, looked warmly into my eyes, stretched out a hand, and made the sign of the cross. I had received her blessing. Officially! Right there in the laundry room of the Don Orione.

I didn't fall to my knees. No vision appeared, nor a voice from the wilderness. And yet her blessing connected with some deep part of my Protestant upbringing. What she'd given me felt welcome, somehow right, and, yes, needed. Though I'd come in a stranger, I felt singled out, and at that moment, special—her blessing a brief beatitude.

I returned to my cab and drove to the front entrance. A woman waiting on a bench outside rose when I pulled up. "Florence Blockel," she offered, and her friendliness soon spread to me.

We'd just emerged from the East Boston tunnel when Florence removed her glasses and produced a handkerchief from her purse. Attached by a wire from the frame of her glasses was an eyeball, a fake one to be sure, but still an eyeball. Good Lord, would you look at that, I said to myself. Though I wanted to ask questions and get a better look, I kept my eyes on the road. I couldn't get a good look or make out the color. Florence cleaned both lenses as if it was all quite normal, and I drove on as if I'd taken lots of passengers with false eyeballs attached to their spectacle frames through the tunnel. When she paid me I noticed that her right eye didn't look quite natural, and I knew why.

I've never forgotten the Lady of the Laundry and Florence Blockel's fake eyeball. Each came into my life unexpectedly and left an indelible mark. Both stirred some life and delight in me. They were reminders that inside my limited world something more waited to be awakened. Surprises did happen. Another life just might lie ahead.

One morning I waited third in line at the Colonnade Hotel on Huntington Avenue. The two cabs ahead of me got radio calls and took off. The bellman came out and motioned me to the door. My fare emerged—a tall, well-dressed, middle-aged man, a little gray around the temples, looking more like he'd take a private limo than a cab. Helped by the doorman, I got the fine-grained leather luggage into the trunk and noted the name on the tag: Robert Tobin. Having been told he was going to Logan, I slid behind the wheel.

It was a nice day, and the airport was a good distance away. The meter advanced rapidly. We began to talk. I always had a few opening lines and probably asked what he'd been doing in Boston. He told me he was chairman of the board of the Opera Company of Boston and had come up from New York for the previous night's production of *La Bohème*. By coincidence, I'd been to the same performance.

All the way we talked about the opera. I've forgotten the names of the principals, but I know we talked of the love duet that ends Act I, about Act II's Latin Quarter scene and Musetta's waltz, and, with a sobbing Rodolfo at her bedside, of Mimi's sad death at the final curtain. It would be pushing it to say that Mr. Tobin and I parted friends, but we enjoyed an enthusiastic conversation.

Three years after my ride with Mr. Tobin, I'd left cab driving and gotten married. I worked as an administrator in a local mental hospital. One night, my wife and I were at the opera. I spotted him during the intermission and walked over. "Hi, Mr. Tobin," I said. "I'm Bill Buffett, your cab driver a few years back. We talked all the way to Logan about *La Bohème*." He lit up and boomed, "I've told more people about how in Boston even the cab drivers are cultured!"

I value the Bible and what I learned at Harvard, but the wisest words I've ever heard about the human condition came from Nick Nicastro, a traffic manager at Checker. After a year of driving, I decided to become a therapist and so I needed to get a master's degree in social work.

One afternoon, Nick and I sat on a bench outside the "executive" offices of Checker Taxi. To prove my current employment, I needed Nick to sign my application to Boston University. He scanned it and asked: "A master's in social work, eh? What are you going to do with it?"

"I'm going to become a therapist," I replied. He responded, "You know who your first customer is going to be, don't you?"

"No, who?"

"Me."

"Ah, Nick," I assured him, "you don't need a therapist."

Nick turned, looked me in the eye, and, taking the ever-present cigar from his mouth, said, "Listen, there isn't a human being on the face of the earth who doesn't need all the help they can get."

Many years later, someone asked about my spiritual education. I said that I'd gotten it driving a cab. Hacking brought me into brief but sometimes intimate contact with all kinds of people. For forty years I'd rubbed shoulders with only the white middle class. Driving a cab, I never knew who would get in or where he or she would want to go. Most trips were routine, but in between there were remarkable fares.

The people I liked came from all walks of life. I learned that poorer people, because they knew the value of a dime, were better tippers. I learned firsthand something that I'd always known theoretically: that good-heartedness and sparkle cut across all races, ages, incomes, and backgrounds.

Now I'm retired and resettled. Like Mrs. Homsey, I have 90 percent of my marbles. Like Philip Baker, I've learned that in marriage there are things you have to overlook, and from Lareda Marshall—"My name means 'victory'"—I learned that sometimes people are what their names mean. And maybe, from driving a cab, I learned to live into my name a bit more.

raised waffles

I found this recipe a few years ago in Marion Cunningham's *Lost Recipes*. She found it in the 1896 edition of the *Fannie Farmer Cookbook*. Even if you think you've found a perfect recipe for waffles, this one will change your mind. Calling it a waffle recipe is like calling a diamond a bright rock.

½ cup warm water, 1 package dry yeast
2 cups warmed milk, 8 tablespoons melted butter (one stick), 1 teaspoon salt,
1 teaspoon sugar, 2 cups flour,
2 eggs, ¼ teaspoon baking soda

1. Use a large mixing bowl (the batter will double in volume). Put the water in the bowl and sprinkle on the yeast. Let stand for 5 minutes. Add the milk, melted butter, salt, sugar, and flour to the yeast mixture and beat until smooth. Cover the bowl with plastic wrap and let stand overnight at room temperature.

2. Just before cooking the waffles, beat in the eggs, add the baking soda, and stir until well mixed. The batter will be very thin. Pour ½ to ¾ cup batter into a hot waffle iron.

Bake 'em until they're golden and crisp. The batter will keep well for several days in the refrigerator.

Own Your Own Life

The glowing review in the *New York Times* caught my attention. I bought *Own Your Own Life,* by the psychiatrist Richard Abell, eager to learn how to own my own life. At forty-two I was unemployed, recently divorced, and living alone in a cabin in western Massachusetts. My two young children lived with their mother in Cambridge, and, despite a recent doctorate from Harvard, I was, as someone said, "a prisoner of myself." I'd applied for several jobs, but nothing had come through. Interviewers probably sensed a sad soul.

My year of living like Thoreau wasn't a complete waste. I occasionally went into Cambridge; my children came out to Colrain on the bus. I entertained a few friends, kept a good-sized garden, cut enough wood to hold me through the winter, sold some potatoes, did some cross-country skiing, and read. It wasn't a bad life, just an unsustainable one.

Life hadn't always been like this. I'd been a high school teacher and for eight years felt I belonged in the classroom. The following three years were less fulfilling. Teaching young people in my twenties and thirties worked well, but I wasn't confident I'd be as effective in my fifties and sixties.

One source of this darkening vision was an older geography teacher whose cubicle was ahead of mine in our social studies office. Between classes she'd sit, head down, snoozing. I imagined myself twenty years later, dozing at my desk, and decided to move on. For a teacher this often means becoming a school administrator, so that became my goal.

I believed that another influence was at work: an unhappy marriage. Maybe a career shake-up would work miracles. With good recommendations but not much enthusiasm, I applied to the Harvard School of Education's Administrative Careers Program (ACP) and was accepted.

In the summer of 1968, my wife and I and our two children packed our station wagon and headed East. We rented a house in Belmont, and in September I joined twenty-five students in the program on opening day. When the school's dean rose before us, he spoke words I've never forgotten: "Welcome to the future leaders of American education."

I heard those words, but they didn't resonate. I felt uninspired, but with nothing else on the horizon, I tried to share my classmates' enthusiasm. I stuck with the program, passed the courses, wrote my thesis, and received a doctorate in the spring of 1972, the same year my wife and I were divorced.

Without much hope, I waited for my next life.

Own Your Own Life offered hope. Abell wrote, "I no longer feel awkward at parties, anxious about what to say. I love parties." He added, "Now I find life exciting, fulfilling."

I, Bill Buffett, was hungry to own my life—especially to enjoy parties and find life exciting.

By contacting the publisher I obtained Abell's address, and directory assistance provided his phone number. I called, made an appointment, and several weeks later headed down Interstate 95 on my way to Abell's home in Riverside, Connecticut.

I knocked on the door of a modest but impressive suburban brick home with flowers and bushes all around it. A stooped and somber older man answered. It was Richard Abell. I'd anticipated a man with a ready smile, a warm greeting, and a twinkle in his eye—a man who found life exciting.

He invited me to accompany him in his car on a few errands. When we returned, I followed him to the basement, where he asked me kneel before a light green ottoman. "Start pounding it," he said. "You need to get out all the anger you've held inside since childhood." I pounded. Then I pounded harder, so hard in fact that I asked, "What happens if I get so mad I throw this through the window?" His succinct response: "Then you'll pay for repairs."

I wondered if other pound-on-command patients had paid for broken glass or lost their composure in a fit of rage. I don't remember other techniques he tried, or what he charged, but I know I never went back. (I tried several other avenues that promised breakthroughs. One was transcendental meditation; another, called est, was the brainchild of Werner Erhard. Neither provided the help I hoped for.)

The acknowledgments page of Abell's book began with a quotation from Tennyson: "I am a part of all I have met." I've met Richard Abell, and I wonder what part of me comes from him. *Own Your Own Life* defines a process and promises excitement and positive experience if that process is followed. If anything, Richard Abell strengthened my suspicion of cure-alls and my distrust of those who claim to have the answer, to have found the way.

More than thirty have passed since I read Abell's book and went to see him. Although I imagine he helped some people, I am not among them. The doctor believes that many people suffer from repressed anger, a result of injunctions like "Don't do that" experienced in childhood. The anger stunts emotional growth and makes people unable to achieve autonomy and intimacy. Many years ago I marked some passages in his book. Abell believes that true growth comes from a "controlled environment for personal growth, such as Transactional Analysis, Gestalt and nonverbal communication groups, in marathons, and in week-long and month-long workshops." He adds, "My experience is that at least

95 percent of the patients who come to work with me change radically, and if they remain in therapy long enough for changes to be ingrained they stay that way."

Abell devotes a fifty-page chapter to a patient called Naomi. Naturally, she is a successful example of his method. It interested me that her story begins in Italy during the war, when the Germans began rounding up Jews. A Gentile friend offers to hide Naomi. She survives the war to eventually become one of the doctor's patients, but I thought of the millions of other Jews who were not so lucky, who weren't offered ownership of their lives.

I also thought of Collin, the dear son of one of my cousins and a cyclist, who recently was struck by a truck and killed. Life is full of contingencies. As someone once said, "We are all temporarily able-bodied." That is a deeper truth than promising people they can own their own lives.

I also thought of the very few who could afford or would have time for Abell's long courses of treatment—such as month-long workshops.

In speaking of one of his patients, Abell says, "A Freudian analyst might have interpreted her fear as a defense against her unconscious desire to kill her own child. This would have been placing ideas in her head that she didn't have at all. It is what Fritz Perls would have called 'mind-fucking.'" Freud's writings are still studied, but not Abell's. I looked on Amazon and found that *Own Your Own Life* is out of print, but there is a new book with that title written by someone else. As I once did, people hunger to own their own lives. The promise sells.

Abell's book concludes, "You can choose to do these things if you want. I choose to do them in order to own my own life."

My primary objection to Abell is his implied view of human nature. He not only doesn't acknowledge other paths to enlightenment; he also fails to speak of the human condition as I know it.

The well-known book *I Never Promised You a Rose Garden* does more than recount a young schizophrenic's struggle for sanity; the title alone tells something of the human condition. Similarly, one therapist called an article about his profession "The Wounded Healer." Abell promises a rose garden and a life free of wounds.

The American writer James Agee acknowledges our wounds. In the introduction to *Many Are Called,* Walker Evans's collection of photographs of riders on New York subways, Agee writes: "They are members of every race and nation on earth. Each is an individual existence, as matchless as a thumbprint or a snowflake. . . . The simplest or the strongest of these beings has been so designed upon by his experience that he has a wound or nakedness to conceal, and guards and disguises by which he conceals it. Scarcely ever, in the whole of his being, are these guards down. Before every other human being . . . something of the mask is there."

Another man who spoke truth is the Greek poet Aeschylus: "He who learns must suffer. And even in our sleep, pain that cannot forget falls drop by drop upon the heart, and in our own despair, against our will, comes wisdom to us by the awful grace of God."

Sometimes I enjoy parties and find life exciting. At other times I am anxious about what to say and am caught up in a routine, dry form of living. Yet I do feel I own more of my life now than I once did. How did it happen? How did I come by a new and better life? I can do no better than Aeschylus. It came by the awful grace of God.

Letters Saved but Hard to Read

The letters, twenty-four of them, are from my father. He has been dead for twenty-five years, but I feel closer to him now at seventy-six than I did when he was alive. We had, not a bad relationship, but a distant one. I loved him as a dutiful son but didn't fall in love with him until after both he and my mother were dead. From a few letters he'd written to her before they married and some excerpts from a dairy he'd kept early in life, I learned that he, too, had struggled.

His letters to me were written in the mid-1970s, when I was in my early forties and my dad had retired from the grocery business. The letters are hand-written. They're hard to read not because of his penmanship but because I hardly recognize the me of thirty-five years ago. I want to say that in a loud and grateful voice. Back then I felt stuck in an unhappy life.

In an old file, I found something I'd written in the early 1970s. Here it is unedited:

A Man at Forty-three

He lives in a one-room, bath attached, studio apartment in Boston's South End. He drives a cab for Checker Taxi, and has a cabin on forty acres of land one hundred miles west of Boston, where he goes on weekends. He has two children, Wendy and Tommy, from a marriage that ended in divorce. He has no real friends. During his life he's been to seven different psychiatrists. He is very lonely and feels most of the time that

his life is coming to an end. He cannot muster the energy to start over.
He recognizes that in him which is engineering his defeat. He loves his
children. He knows he is weak, he wallows in despair and self-pity—his
almost exclusive reality is that of his own feelings. The world and its people
exist faintly as a realm of possibility, but mainly as a source of fear
and shame.

While my life was on hold, my retired father was moving on. My parents' marriage was solid and loving. They were nearing their fiftieth anniversary. He had worked in Buffett's grocery store for forty years, six days a week, twelve hours a day. After his dad died, my father became the go-to guy for more than thirty employees. A columnist for the local newspaper once named him "the friendliest man in Omaha." My dad was a good bowler and a better-than-average golfer. He and my mother traveled to Switzerland in the summer and to Death Valley, California, in the winter. Twice a year they would drive to my cabin in western Massachusetts.

During one of these visits, I asked them to come to Boston. I was in group therapy at the time and arranged with the leader, Dr. Lee Birk, for the four of us to meet together. From various therapists I'd absorbed the message that my parents were responsible for my problems, and I hoped for a breakthrough. Though none came, I remember my father saying that he'd had a problem with stuttering, a problem I hadn't known about. I also remember Dr. Birk saying after they'd gone: "You know, your parents are pretty nice people."

In his letters, excerpts from which I reprint below, my father spoke about what he and my mother were doing, about my children, and about his relationship with me.

Still no rain here in Omaha—15 days of dry weather and some days have been very hot. My six tomato plants still look good but no tomatoes set on when it is this hot and dry.

Your last letter was another step in our understanding each other and I hope that this letter will be another step—step-by-step we will come closer together until some of your anger toward us will fade away. I know that most of my angers toward you have faded, as I understand your problems. Let me ask you, Bill, if you did not think that some of Wendy and Tommy's problems are not your problems. As a parent do you not like to help your children with their problems and troubles? Your mother and I feel the same about your problems. One of your problems is your anger toward us that we can help you solve.

As for my reaction to your taking the asparagus and stove to New York— five or three or one minute after I made the remark I knew that it was none of my business to throw cold water on your idea. What flashed through my mind was a 41-year-old, good-looking gentleman carrying a cardboard box into a fancy hotel lobby. It was a unique idea and I am very glad that you let the old man's word go in one ear and out the other.

Another time was in Massachusetts when your grain-grinding mill went on the floor—I shot off my mouth without thinking and was sorry afterward that I didn't keep my trap shut.

Maybe some of your anger toward us is because of our shortcomings. We are not as smart as some people. I am sure that you want other people to overlook some of your shortcomings. One of my shortcomings is putting things off to a later date or never getting them done until it is too late. Fritz's shortcoming is when he did not call you when he said he would. He just put it off and the days went by. [Fritz was my brother.]

We are very glad that your group meetings seem to be going along to your advantage. Problems—problems, problems everybody has problems; a lot of people have problems that are no different than yours or mine. Many of my problems I still have; some I have been able to solve and some I have been able to ignore and forget about. I can't solve all the problems of my physical body or my mental body, but I do find some relief when I call on my spiritual body for help. I hope that this is not preaching in your mind. You are different than I and what helps me may not help you.

You speak of your feeling of worthlessness. Is that not a product of your imagination? In my book you are very far from worthless—with all your energy and brains you are a bright man with lots of past angers and a great future.

With lots of love, Dad
P.S. Don't forget we need your love.

May 30, 1974; Omaha

While in Chicago I cut Fritz's front lawn and did a little painting for Pam. I enjoyed cutting the lawn and doing the other things back at your place. Kath or I did not enjoy the flies and for three days after leaving your place I still had a couple of bites that bothered me. I hope that they are not bothering you too much.

Katherine and I were very glad that we had the talks at your cabin about your personal problems. We were very sorry to hear about them and it hurt our hearts, but to share your problems makes us feel much closer to our son that we love. We want to share your joys but also your problems. We feel by knowing your problems we are closer to you and hopefully we with our prayers and counsel can help you in the days to come.

Dr. Birk seemed to be a very fine fellow. From our short visit with him he seems to have his feet on the ground and a lot different than I thought he would be. If he can help you only you can tell. I do not want to preach but as he said you have to keep your mind off of the negative things in your past life and think about all the positive things that you have going for you. You have done us a favor by bringing to our attention many of our shortcomings for which we are thankful.

"And how does your garden grow?" I sure enjoyed working with you on Stetson Road. [My cabin was on Stetson Road in Colrain, Massachusetts.] *I feel closer to you than I have in years.*

JUNE 12, 1974; OMAHA

I know that this is the 12th because tomorrow is the 13th of June, your mother's birthday.

It seems to me that I thought that I knew you but now I know that I did not know you. Probably a lot of that is my fault but you will have to take some of the blame. During high school and college we glowed in your honors and achievements. You and Fritz are dear to us.

JULY 17, 1974; OMAHA

I really don't know what to say or just how to say it in this letter, but just let us talk about anger for a few minutes—of course I will be doing all the talking but I sure do not want to sound like I am preaching.

Your angers can probably be classified into several different groups. Anger at yourself, anger with yourself—anger with your family—anger with other people—anger with things around you (bugs in the garden, tractors that don't start, etc.). These last angers you might as well forget for you can do nothing about them.

Any anger at yourself and anger with yourself are probably pretty much alike but there must be some difference—your old pops would have a hard time to separate them. Many times I have been angry with myself. It is just as natural as the sun coming up in the east. Don't you think that Nixon has been angry with himself for some of the dumb things he has done? (And the whole country can see his mistakes.)

Anger with your family is somewhat natural—you love them—they are part of you and you want them to be perfect in your eyes. No one is perfect. Everyone has his or her own mind and every mind works a little different. Anger within a family can split it apart—let's not let anger split our family. I think that my anger toward you, Bill, has lessened the last two months and has been replaced with much more love. Understanding and love will easily replace anger if you give them a chance.

Anger with other people will not hurt them but only tear you apart. A forgiving person will enjoy life more and have many more friends than a person who has angers and keeps them.

What I say to you in this letter applies to any person. Always remember that you, Bill, and Fritz and your families are part of us and our love will never die.

AUGUST 1, 1974; OMAHA

The weather here is more of the same. Hot, hot, and hot days with night temperatures about 75°. We have had the air conditioner going many nights and of course during the days. No clouds, no rain and no moisture in the forecast. There has been no general rain since June 10.

Went to church Sunday A.M. and the preacher talked about fences and gates. You and I have both built a fence between us with only a small gate and that has been closed most of the time. If we can continue to make the gate longer and to keep it open, I think we will be much happier and our love will be able to be carried back and forth with ease. They showed a movie with the service that showed a man with a fence around his house. He threw a brick over the fence and a brick was thrown back—he throws over more bricks and got more bricks back—after that had gone on for some time he threw a flower (daisy) over the fence and soon lots of daisies were coming over the fence to him. I guess that is the way life is—a person generally gets back about what he gives out.

At the end of the service some of the young people passed out daisies to all the members of the congregation.

AUGUST 8, 1974; OMAHA

Received your letter yesterday and was glad to note that your garden seems to be progressing in fine style.

Well, I suppose that you heard Nixon last night and again this morning. We listened to the speech on NBC TV. A person cannot help but have mixed feelings about what has happened. Can you imagine the feelings of the actors that are on the stage? My heart goes out for Nixon's family and also Ford's family.

I thought that Nixon did a good job in his farewell speech and I thought that the TV newsmen were very good in their remarks after the talks. They are now talking about the Honeymoon in Washington—I hope that it will last and our elected members of Congress can now get on with the job of running the country—goodness knows there are plenty of problems that need to be solved that they should have been working on instead of taking all of their energy on Watergate.

This has been a great day for us here in Nebraska—it has finally rained. We have had good rains throughout the state with more on the way. June 10 to August 8 is a long time without rain.

Since talking to you Saturday eve, I have been reading more in your book "All the President's Men." It sure is good reading and a book everyone should read. I think that I will give it to Tom Henshaw to read when I have finished. Thank you for talking to me about it and insisting on my reading it. It sure took a lot of digging by those reporters.

DECEMBER 17, 1974; OMAHA

We know that you will have a great time with your two children this weekend getting the Christmas tree. I wish I were there. But as we get older the cold weather appeals to us less and less.

At this time of the year our minds go back to all the good times at past Christmas's. When you were in grade school—then high school—and then when you would come home from college. Lots of fun and lots of good food. I am sure that in the years ahead you will look back with the same memories with Wendy and Tommy. What you do with them and for them will not be forgotten.

We will be calling you this weekend out at the cabin so we hope that the phone is in working order. Thinking of you many times each day with lots of love and prayers.

MARCH 1976; DEATH VALLEY

We are trying to keep in shape so that we will be able to replenish your woodpile this summer. You undoubtedly put a pretty good hole in it this past weekend. Mother will drag in the small stuff and I will split the big wood. There is nothing like a good wood fire on a cold day.

It was good to talk to Wendy, Tommy and you. Tom seems to be able to express himself better all the time. Wendy was our first grandchild and will always have a close place to our hearts. Just in a few short years she will probably want to fly from the nest. Such is life and there is no way to make time stand still.

Your letters about your family are always so interesting. Something new each day. I hope that each day you help someone over one of life's hurdles. They are so big to them and your job is to give them a little push.

Your last letter to us was quite a letter. You sure have the ability to write in a good strong way. Your problems with Mary cause us a good deal of worry and we wish that we could do something to help you. It is one of those problems that there is no right answer but we hope that the best answer will come out of the troubles. Whatever the future holds we hope that the children will come out of it in good shape. Maybe the children should be in on the meetings between you and Mary. They may have ideas that would help you both.

October 8, 1976; Omaha

We enjoyed our two talks with you over the weekend. It really gives us a lift to talk to you and find you in good spirits. And the crowning lift for us was at the tail end of the talk yesterday when you told us that you loved us. We know that you love us but to hear you say it means a great deal to us. We love you and always will and we hope that we show it. You and your children are always in our prayers.

I know that you do not like your cab job. Many days I did not like my job at the store—long hours of hard work—putting up with employees and customers. So many times there was no right answer. So often I would wake up in the middle of the night trying to solve some of the problems from the day before. Verbal fights between employees. Some employees I probably should have fired but maybe the next one would be worse. I could go on and on but somehow we were able to pay our bills and close the store with a little left in the pocket.

You speak of your depressions—I think that that is only normal with any human being. Some people's depressions are worse than others. Under-

standably yours are worse than mine. When I have one I have to take my mind off of my depressions and have to start thinking of all the good things the world (the Lord) has given me. My health and a fairly good mind are two of the best. I'll bet if you would write down all the good things that you have going for you the list would be plenty long. Health— good mind—two wonderful children—love of opera—the list could go on and on. I hope that this does not sound like preaching. I will close now and promise I will write more often.

DECEMBER 1976; OMAHA

I can well remember December 7 some years ago working at the store when we heard that the Japs had bombed Pearl Harbor. It is cold and raw here now and I can remember working with the Christmas trees and what a cold job that was, with the wind blowing and the snow falling. Trying to sell all the Christmas candy and gift items. Long hours on the job but I did enjoy my work but I am over the hill as far as working time and worrying like I did at one time. It was a lot of work but a lot of fun at the same time.

In your letter when you told about getting some of the history of your cabin was very interesting. Every time I go in your basement and see all the stone works I can not help but marvel as to how they got them all in place. And to think that they did not have tractors or all the heavy equipment that people have today. They must have had stronger backs and lots of time and strong horses to do the job. Do you suppose that the moonshine operation was an old fashioned still or were they just making applejack at your place? [Two other buildings that had stood on the same foundation as my cabin were a dry goods store and a place that made moonshine.]

I am glad to know that Tommy is doing good in school. You say that spelling is one of his better subjects—that is something that he does not get from his grandfather on his dad's side. I have always been very poor at spelling. I was poor in spelling in grade school—high school and still am. Alveria Anderson who used to be our maid and worked at the store was about the poorest speller I have known. She had a tough time spelling apple or cabbage. Every one does not have the same ability in everything.

We are looking forward to Christmas with great joy. Let's hope that the weather stays reasonably good and we stay in good health. I know that we will have a great time.

JANUARY, 1977; DEATH VALLEY

This has been another perfect day in Death Valley. No wind no clouds the temp about 68° for the high. We have had practically no wind this year so far. We will probably get some in February and the first part of March. When the wind blows it really fills the air with dust and sand.

Your letters about all your children are sure interesting. [Late in 1976, I got a job as the director of a psychiatric halfway house on Leonard Avenue in Cambridge. "Your children" refers to the residents of the house.] *Every one of your children is different and has their own problems. You know, Bill, if you get them all well that you will be out of a job. Ha! Being around the people at Leonard Ave. cannot help but help you. I know that you have problems with them that I would have one hell of a time to try to solve. It must take a lot of time and understanding. The people out here could use some counseling, all they do is gripe, gripe and more gripe. But they all have their good sides and we run across a lot of top-notch people. I will never forget one of the customers coming in the store and saying to me that the easiest thing in the world to do is complain.*

FEBRUARY 1977; DEATH VALLEY

It is nice to have a son that gets the old man's mind stirred up a little. You gave me a little flak on using the word "peace." According to the pocket dictionary that we have out here, "peace" means "An agreement to end a war. A state of quiet calm. Harmony in personal relations." No, this life does not offer peace to anyone and it is a state of mind that you or I will probably never attain in this life, but I can offer it to you and maybe you will come a little closer to "peace." Peace between nations and individuals can be attained but peace within myself is something that I try to work for.

Our leader at church this morning talked about "Fruits of the Spirit" from Galatians 5:22: "But the fruit of the spirit is love, joy, peace, long-suffering, gentleness, goodness and faith."

Your comments about working at the Cambridge Co-op were very interesting. It must be some place to do that much business. I was surprised that they would have fresh strawberries at this time of year. Do you remember how I would get you up to go to the store and shovel the snow off the front sidewalk? And how we would go to Market? There is not even a market in Omaha to go to anymore. When I first started going to market with your grandfather, there were as many horse and wagons as there were automobiles.

MARCH 14, 1977; DEATH VALLEY

We received your letter today and are very glad that you are feeling better after feeling depressed for a week or two. We wish that we could help you in some way. Have you tried reading the Bible for a lift? There is a good lot in the Bible that does everyone some good.

We hope that you had a good time at the cabin this last weekend. We tried to phone you but got no answer. It will not be long before the grass starts to get green in your front yard and the birds will be singing. Your children are very lucky to have that cabin to go to even though sometimes they probably get a little tired of going out there.

From your letter it seems that you enjoy working at the Co-op. That probably goes back to the days when you helped at the store. I, also, enjoy a good piece of raw beef. It has a flavor all its own. I can remember you taking pieces of raw beef at the store and eating it.

DECEMBER 2, 1977; OMAHA

We are very happy for you, Susan, Wendy and Tom. We had a great time at your wedding. Ames, Iowa will always be remembered as a place of good times and happy memories to us.

I don't know of any more news that we can't talk about over the phone. We are so happy for you and Susan. Wendy and Tom are a joy to us as they grow up to be a nice young woman and a great young man with you and Susan for guidance.

MAY 5, 1978; CHICAGO

We are planning on leaving here Sunday noon and will probably arrive at the cabin late Tuesday or Wednesday morn. We hope that the weather is nice for our drive back and that it warms up at the cabin. It has been cold and windy here in Chicago.

We are all feeling better here at Fritz's house. Sarah is going to be in an ice show this evening. Maku and I are going tomorrow evening. Sunday morn we will all go to church.

The past two weeks have been hard on all of us and we know that you, Susan, Wendy and Tom have suffered with us. [My niece Rebecca Buffett, Fritz and Pam's younger daughter, died following heart surgery at the Mayo Clinic.] *Things are getting brighter with the passing of time. Time heals but a person still has a wound.*

JANUARY 3, 1979 (the last letter I have from him)

1978 has come and gone. It has been a year of good and bad. It started out with me in the hospital for 2 weeks and then in April we lost Rebecca, which was very hard to take, but we had her for 7 good years and lots of enjoyment from her.

For you I cannot help but think it was a good year. Getting a very good wife (Susan) was wonderful and the growth of your two children gives Maku and me great pleasure. Your trip to Greece was another plus for 1978.

A Man at Seventy-six

He lives in a recently remodeled home in Arlington, Massachusetts. He is retired and has a cabin on forty acres of land one hundred miles west of Boston where he and Susan, his wife of over thirty years, will go often in the future. He has three children, Wendy and Tom from his first marriage, and Noah, the son he has with Susan. He has many friends. During his life, he has had many lives. He enjoys the companionship of his wife and many others and feels most of the time that life is rich and joyful. He has the energy to continue a life that is filled with rewards and opportunities. He recognizes that in him which is grateful and moving forward. He loves his wife, his children, his grandchildren, and many others. He knows he is blessed; he relishes life in its endless variety and abundance. The world and its people exist as a source of satisfaction, but mainly as a source of life and wonder.

great goo

I can recommend with enthusiasm every recipe in the book but this one. Wendy, Tommy, and I gave it this name many years ago, and I haven't made it since. Not that it tastes bad, but times have changed since we made it on winter nights at our cabin in Colrain. They took the bus out to Greenfield from their mother's house in Cambridge every other weekend. I would meet them, and we'd drive to the cabin. Sometimes it was bitter cold, and I was anxious to get to our little home in the woods and stoke the fires, not only to keep us warm but also to whip up a batch of Great Goo.

⅓ cup vinegar
⅓ cup any sweet liquid
(such as syrup drained from pineapple)
½ cup brown sugar
1 tablespoon soy sauce
3 teaspoons cornstarch
¼ cup water

combine vinegar, liquid, brown sugar, and soy sauce and whisk in a saucepan over medium heat.

shake together cornstarch and water in a small jar and slowly add to the vinegar mixture.

cook until the mixture is clear and boil for about 1 minute.

add chopped cooked celery, onion, green pepper, and meat and ½ cup peanuts.

serve over rice.

Darwin

I'm seventy-six years old and I have always assumed that as people aged, body and passion both slowed down. Bodies sure do; but passion? Not necessarily.

Passions? Here are mine: Charles Darwin, King Tut, the Houghton *Shahnameh*, opera, the Boston Red Sox, Carleton College, and Nebraska. A diverse group, belonging—most probably—only to me, like my unique face and fingerprints.

Sexual passion is there, but subdued and without as much energy as it once had. A loss? Sure. But in its place is a deeper love of my wife, family, and friends—and of life itself. It is a love that's neither passing nor diffuse, and it is something that brightens each of my days.

No passion remains at fever pitch. But each of mine has staying power and flows deep inside. In college I majored in philosophy, but I rarely recall specifics from my studies except for the French philosopher Henri Bergson's concept of élan vital. In English translations, the phrase appears as "vital impetus," which exactly defines my passions. They have enriched my inner life and provided a vital impetus to engage with the world.

Charles Darwin entered my life in the spring of 1966, during my eighth year of teaching history at New Trier High School. One day the department head asked if I wanted to work for a year at Harvard University on curriculum development. "Absolutely," I said. By fall, my wife, children, and I were settled in an apartment in Cambridge, and I began my task.

Our assignment was to develop a course for high school students about the impact of science on society. Rather than create a survey course, we would select three themes from nineteenth-century England and devote significant time to each. They were the invention of the steam engine and its influence, the city of Manchester and how industrialization changed it, and the unit to which I was assigned, Darwin and his impact on society.

A scholar guided each unit. My leader was E. O. Wilson, a Harvard zoologist. He was a smart old shoe, and his enthusiasm was contagious. I had neither training in biology nor any idea that a nineteenth-century naturalist would become one of the passions of my life. Taking a year to focus on a great man and having Wilson as my guide both fueled my enthusiasm.

In Darwin's time almost everyone in the Western world believed in the biblical story of creation, as revealed in Genesis. God created all species of plants and animals, including Adam and Eve. They hadn't changed since the beginning of time. God put a cow, a frog, a petunia, and an oak tree on earth, looking just as they do now.

Darwin also believed this biblical version when, at the age of twenty-two, he got a chance to sail as the naturalist aboard the H.M.S. *Beagle*. Its government-funded mission? To improve maps of South America's coast and get better readings on longitude by sailing around the world.

Earlier in his life Darwin had tried medical school, but it didn't take; he then decided to study for the ministry. At this point the opportunity to join the *Beagle* expedition came along. Darwin always had a keen interest in nature, so the opportunity seemed perfect. His theological studies could wait until he returned. The *Beagle* sailed on December 27, 1831, and returned to England five years later on October 2, 1836.

On his long voyage, Darwin spent hours riding on horseback, climbing high hills, walking through forests, and visiting islands. He observed nature and slowly began to see things in a radically different way. He returned to England with pages of notes, and, in glass jars and tubes, more than a thousand specimens to add to those he'd already mailed.

After his return Darwin wrote what he called a "sketch" of his ideas, but he put it in a drawer. *On the Origin of Species* wasn't published for twenty-three years. Why did he wait so long? Darwin knew his ideas about the development of life opposed the common belief and the teachings of the Church. Everyone assumed that what we saw had always been there. After all, as the Bible says: "And God created. . ." The belief was held with such conviction that, referring to his idea that species evolve, Darwin said, "It is almost like committing murder."

This sounds strange to our ears, but "murder" says a lot about how radically at odds Darwin's idea was with the teaching of the Church, an institution that held greater sway over people's minds in his day than it does today. To argue against creationism, Darwin knew, would upset many people, including his devout wife Emma. In the introduction to the *Origin* Darwin writes: "The view which most naturalists entertain, and which I formerly entertained—namely that each species has been independently created—is erroneous. I am fully convinced that species are not immutable." This, he knew, was a bombshell.

An important event in 1858 caused Darwin to take the sketch from his drawer and begin writing immediately. He'd received a letter from a fellow naturalist named Alfred Russel Wallace, at work in the South Seas. Wallace expressed ideas about species development similar to Darwin's own. If Charles delayed publication, he risked being preempted by Wallace.

On August 12, 1859, *On the Origin of Species* went on sale in London bookstores. All 1,250 copies were sold by the end of the day. People were curious but highly doubtful that species could change so dramatically.

Darwin expected this reaction. It is why he referred to his book as "one long argument." He knew he must convince a skeptical public. Surprisingly, he begins with a chapter about pigeons. In Darwin's day, pigeon fanciers were as common as dog breeders are today. Different breeds of dogs look radically different from each other. The same is true of pigeons.

An illustration in the *Origin* shows some of the more than three hundred varieties of pigeons that breeders created over many years. The Jacobean looks radically different from the Fantail, which looks very different from the Pouter. They are all descendents of the rock pigeon. Darwin is saying, look what man has done over a few hundred years; think of what nature can do over millions. He wanted people to question the belief that species haven't changed. If man can alter pigeons, imagine what nature can do with a flower, a weed, or an elk—in fact, with every single species of flora and fauna.

Darwin knew that species can change, but the big question was how. First, he knew that within species many more seeds and eggs are produced than can survive. Ed Wilson pointed this out in a dramatic way in the high school science curriculum produced by our unit: "A female codfish lays 85,000,000 eggs at once. Suppose a single pair of codfish and their descendents were allowed to reproduce freely in the Atlantic Ocean. In just three years, a person could walk from the U.S. to England on the backs of their solidly packed offspring. Yet fish reproduce at a slow rate compared to bacteria. Imagine that a single bacterium, too small to be seen with the naked eye, is placed on the floor. Suppose we allow it and its descendents to reproduce without hindrance, requiring them only to remain in a space one foot square. If we were to return in just 48 hours, the offspring of this single bacterium would form a solid column passing up through the earth's atmosphere and growing beyond the solar system at the speed of light."

Wilson also focused on the mustard plant: "Consider a mustard plant. It produces about 730,000 seeds annually, which, if they all took root and matured, in two years would occupy an area 2,000 times that of the land surface of the earth." Clearly, species produce more offspring than can survive.

Darwin was familiar with Thomas Malthus's *Essay on the Principle of Population*. Population growth, Malthus argued, far outstrips the earth's ability to provide for all. Darwin combined this idea with the fact that each individual varies slightly from other members of a species. (I've always been struck by how most cows and all robins look alike—more or less. However, looks deceive. These creatures differ from each other as much as humans do. No two of us are alike, and the same is true of robins, dandelions, and sheep.) Although man is able to gain some control over his food supply, no other species can. Within each species, there is a struggle to survive. Slight variation makes some better able to survive than others.

Darwin hit upon the idea that nature decided who would prevail. Variation, a struggle for existence, natural selection—these were the key ideas of Darwin's theory of evolution. New species bearing a resemblance to their ancestors would appear. Darwin's genius was to realize that over long periods of time, incredible changes could occur.

In anticipation of the many arguments against his theory, Darwin performed experiments to support his findings. My favorite concerns his response in the *Origin* to someone who raised this question: "A species of cactus on the Galapagos is similar to one on the mainland of South America. Since salt water kills seeds, how could they travel over 500 miles of ocean? Doesn't it make more sense to believe that God had created two similar but different species—placing one on an island and one on the continent?"

Darwin relates an experiment he conducted in his back yard: "In the course of two months, I picked up in my garden twelve kinds of seeds out of the excrement of small birds and some of them germinated. But the following fact is more important: the crops of birds do not secrete gastric juices, and do not in the least injure, as I know by trial, the germination of seeds; now after a bird has devoured a large supply of food, all the grains do not pass into the gizzard for twelve or even eighteen hours. A bird in this interval might easily be blown to the distance of 500 miles." This is but one of many experiments Darwin described in the *Origin*.

It is fitting that the last words in this section come from my two mentors: Wilson and Darwin. Wilson wrote: "It is a tribute to Darwin that after over 100 years, the *Origin* remains a good elementary introduction to evolutionary theory. Modern biologists have been able to answer questions that Darwin could not answer, and in support of his position they have added new evidence that amounts in itself to a whole new branch of biology; but Darwin's basic idea remains unchanged."

Here is the last paragraph from Charles Darwin's *On the Origin of Species:* "It is interesting to contemplate an entangled bank, clothed with plants of many kinds, with birds singing in the bushes, with various insects flitting about, and with worms crawling through the damp earth, and to reflect that these elaborately constructed forms, so different from each other, and dependent on each other in so complex a manner, have all been produced by laws acting around us . . . thus, from the war of nature, from famine and death, the most exalted object which we are capable of conceiving, namely the production of the higher animals, directly follows. There is grandeur in this view of life, with its several powers, having been originally breathed into a few forms or into one; and that, whilst this planet has gone cycling on according to the fixed law of gravity, from so simple a beginning endless forms most beautiful and wonderful have been, and are being, evolved."

Passions have staying power. They survive. Like everything alive, they evolve. At various times, I've been interested in geology, party politics, and Lincoln logs. Lincoln logs no longer fascinate me; politics and geology engage me but aren't passions. Only a few of the thousands of tiny seeds that eventually drift from a flower survive to become dandelions; so it is with passions. We encounter a myriad of things in life, but only a few become passions.

When I returned to New Trier I was full of Darwin, and my Modern European History classes showed his influence. The course still began with England's Glorious Revolution in the seventeenth century, but whereas previously Darwin had received only passing mention, now students who took Mr. Buffett's revised history class studied evolution for four weeks.

One day the department head got a call from the parent of one of my students complaining that her daughter hadn't learned anything about the Revolutions of 1848. He laughed and didn't take it seriously.

A few years ago I had lunch with an old colleague who had stayed at New Trier. I told him how much I appreciated being trusted to teach what I wanted. Reflecting contemporary education's emphasis on standardized tests, my friend commented, "Oh, you couldn't do that anymore." I remembered the wise words of our superintendent: "The most important thing teachers teach is themselves," which is what I was doing with my heart-afire emphasis on Charles Darwin.

Six years ago, my wife and I took a train from London south to Orphington. From there, we hired a taxi for the short trip to Down House, where Darwin lived with his wife, Emma, and their ten children. Here he kept and studied the specimens and notes he'd accumulated on the *Beagle*. Here he took long walks, thought about the evidence, and wrote the *Origin*.

At Down House, a large family room occupies the first floor, along with a replica of the study where Darwin worked. On the second, display cases show the basics of his idea of evolution. Outside, the lawn, gardens, and path—where he walked and studied orchids, worms, and birds—remain the same.

I think of the trip to Down House as a pilgrimage, a venture that reflected and fed my curiosity about the great man.

On a small rock in my office are some barnacles, those common little things in white shells that get in the way and are usually ignored. I used to find them annoying too, until I read *Darwin and the Barnacles* by Rebecca Stott. I learned some amazing things. On the coast of South America, Darwin found small holes inside a conch shell. In each lived a tiny creature. Under his microscope, Darwin found that they resembled barnacles, but he knew that barnacles made their own shells. He sought sample barnacles from naturalists all over the world. He spent five years on his study and eventually published four volumes about barnacles, all before writing and publishing the *Origin*. That fact never ceases to amaze me. Five years on barnacles! What passion! His work did have an important payoff. By the time the *Origin* hit the bookstores, Darwin had established his reputation as an accomplished naturalist. Colleagues knew to take him seriously.

My own interest in barnacles led to a personal disaster. My wife and I were on an Alaskan cruise. One day on the dock of a small village, a naturalist on our boat pointed out some barnacles on one of the pilings. I mentioned that I knew something about them and would be willing to give a talk. Our ship had several naturalists, and it was unusual for a layman to encroach on their turf. The old adage "Fools rush in where angels fear to tread" would have stood me in good stead.

That afternoon on a back deck, the passengers gathered. I was told I had ten minutes, so my introduction was brief. With mike in hand, I spoke, confident that the audience was mesmerized by my passion for barnacles. I explained that because barnacles were hermaphrodites they needed to cluster together in order to procreate, and that wherever a barnacle landed, it stayed for life. To give my talk some spice, I delighted in revealing that, relative to their size, barnacles have the longest penises of any living organism.

Expounding enthusiastically, I lost track of time. Nearly thirty minutes after I'd begun, one of the naturalists knelt frantically before me and made a "time's up" sign. I ended quickly. Later I learned that my embarrassed wife had already retired to our cabin. The incident cast a pall over the trip. I remember it well.

I have happier memories of another part of the path on which Darwin has taken me. In 1995 I went with my family on a trip to the Galapagos Islands, an important stop on Darwin's trip around the world. One day I asked our ship's captain to take us near the island called Daphne Major, the setting for Jonathan Weiner's book *The Beak of the Finch*. Darwin had mentioned finches in the *Origin*; thirteen species have now been identified on the islands. Weiner writes about the Grants, a couple from Princeton, who had been coming to Daphne for twenty years to observe the birds.

"Observe" doesn't do justice to the story. The Grants have captured, tagged, and measured thousands of finches. They know individual finches by sight and have given them names. Finches vary, if ever so slightly. The number of finches varies from year to year. Some years there are a few hundred, other years nearly a thousand. Rainfall and other factors determine how many are born and how many die. Nature selects the fittest. They survive. By tracking weather and the finches, the Grants have been able to document changes within each species and relate them to changes in the environment. They've been able to see at first hand what Darwin never did: evolution in action.

The introductory paragraph to the *Origin* reads: "When on board H.M.S. *Beagle,* as naturalist, I was much struck with certain facts in the distribution of the inhabitants of South America, and in the geological relations of the present to the past inhabitants of that continent. These facts seemed to me to throw some light on the origin of species—that mystery of mysteries, as it has been called by one of our greatest philosophers."

About religion, Darwin wrote a fellow naturalist, "My theology is a simple muddle. I cannot look at the Universe as the result of blind chance, yet I can see no evidence of beneficent Design." I, too, see no evidence of beneficent Design and I share Darwin's muddle. But what he has given me—a sense of awe at all creation—means far more.

Darwin referred to the Galapagos as "the origin of all my views." It's fitting that so much relevant and revelatory research continues on these rugged bits of land.

My views, thanks to Darwin, led me to E. O. Wilson and his fascination with ants. In his first major work, *Journey to the Ants,* written with Bert Hölldobler, Wilson writes: "Our passion is ants. . . . When combined, all ants in the world taken together weigh about as much as all human beings. . . . Only 13,500 species of highly social insects are known, 9,500 of which are ants, out of a grand total of 750,000 insect species that have been recognized to date by biologists. Thus more than half the living tissue of insects is made up of just two percent of the species, the fraction that live in well-organized colonies. . . . In a nearby locality we identified 43 species from a single tree. . . . Ants arose amidst the dinosaurs about a hundred million years ago and spread quickly around the world."

Though he's published many other books, two of which have won Pulitzer Prizes, ants remain his great interest. On a recent *NOVA* episode titled "Lord of the Ants," Wilson remarked, "I can't understand why everyone isn't fascinated by ants." I can't, either.

Once, while on a panel of Harvard professors, Wilson said that the question he is asked most often is, "I've got ants in my kitchen. What should I do?" He responded, "I tell these folks to get down on their hands and knees and watch carefully. See where they go, what they seem to be looking for, what happens when they meet another ant."

On a trip to the Amazon a few years ago, I took a picture of some leaf-cutter ants, each carrying a piece of leaf bigger than itself. The leaves aren't eaten but are carried to the nest and chewed into a paste on which a fungus grows. It's the fungus that the ants eat. Unlike my fellow travelers, all birders, I found ants more interesting. Once I sat on a log by myself, simply to be in the quiet surrounded by tall trees and thick foliage. After I got up, I saw tiny red ants crawling on my arms. They didn't bite and were soon gone. I read later that in the Amazon one should never lean against a tree or sit on a log. The reason: ants are everywhere, and some are poisonous.

Sitting at my computer recently, I watched an ant amble by. I didn't squish him. He would never know that my benign response had its origin in 1966, the year I spent as a curriculum developer in Cambridge, Massachusetts.

The Houghton *Shahnameh*

I'm often surprised but rarely shocked when I read a newspaper. Early on a fall day in 1976, however, sitting in my Checker taxi in front of Boston's Lenox Hotel, I was enjoying a doughnut, hot coffee, a cigarette, and the *New York Times* while waiting in the taxi line. I saw a short article. Arthur Houghton was putting up for sale, through Christie's of London, some pages of the *Shahnameh* he'd owned since 1959. The news devastated me.

Why did the article stand out? The reason goes back to the fall of 1972, when I was wandering through the Metropolitan Museum of Art in New York City. Rounding a corner, I came upon an exhibit with several waist-high glass cases full of miniature paintings called "A King's Book of Kings." I'd never seen anything like them. Where did they come from? Who painted them?

In vivid colors, the miniatures revealed a new and entrancing world: wild beasts, lovers, flowers, trees, decorative interiors, rocky crags, vicious battles, pastoral scenes, courtiers and princesses, warriors and wooers. Each painting had an explanation. Beneath one, *The Court of Gayumarth,* I read: "Gayumarth, the first King of Iran, ruled the world from a mountaintop. During his thirty-year reign the arts of life originated: food was discovered and people made clothing of animal skins. Cattle and wild beasts became tame before Gayumarth's craggy throne, which men approached with reverence."

The painting shows Gayumarth, seated on an earthen throne, surrounded by animals and courtiers in a lush, natural environment. It is an exquisite scene, in breathtaking color: calm, gentle, and harmonious.

I learned that the paintings were part of a book called the *Shahnameh,* a work of art from sixteenth-century Persia. The text, written by the poet Firdowsi, told the country's history from its mythic beginnings to the Muslem conquest. Artists had illustrated the book much as artists might illustrate stories from the Bible or the *Odyssey.* For brushes, the artists used the fur of kittens and baby squirrels.

Arthur Houghton, a wealthy philanthropist and trustee of the Metropolitan, owned the book and had recently given the museum 78 of the 258 paintings in the original work. His gift had occasioned the exhibition. I stayed in New York an extra day in order to see it again. I bought a book titled *A King's Book of Kings,* published in conjunction with the exhibit and written by the curator of Indian and Islamic art at Harvard University's Fogg Art Museum, Stuart Carey Welch.

When I got home, I read more. Shah Ima'il commissioned this *Shahnameh* in 1522 as a gift to his son, Prince Tahmasp. Materials and artists were assembled. Work went on for several years. The leader of the project, the artist Sultan Muhammad, supervised others and painted several of the illustrations himself. A review of the exhibit in *Time* magazine noted, "If Persian art were as well known in this country as Western art, Sultan Muhammad's name would rank with Michelangelo's as one of the great artists in human history."

Though the history of the *Shahnameh* from about 1540 until 1800 is uncertain, its excellent condition suggests that the book was treated with great care. By 1800 it had arrived at the Royal Ottoman Library in Istanbul. In 1903 it appeared at an exhibition of Islamic art in Paris. The lender and presumed owner was Baron Edmond de Rothschild. A catalog for the 1903 exhibit referred to the *Shahnameh* as "the most precious book here with few equals anywhere."

I learned that Stuart Carey Welch knew that the Rothschild family was selling the *Shahnameh.* At about the same time, he heard that Arthur

Houghton was interested in purchasing a major work of art. Welch arranged for the sale, and, sometime later, the two of them sat in the anteroom of a New York art dealer, watching as the large book was wheeled in.

"It is a heavy book, almost too big to handle, intended for special occasions, pretentious but entertaining," wrote Welch in *A King's Book of Kings*. "The smooth binding is warmly, solidly patinated by time and handling. The cover opens like a massive, well-oiled door. The dry, mellowed pages, thin but firm, crackle pleasantly as one turns them."

As they leafed through these exquisite pages, Welch looked for an illustration of people clothed in leopard skins. The painting he sought, *The Court of Gayumarth,* is referred to in a 1546 account of past and present Persian painters. Sultan Muhammad is referred to as the "Zenith of the Age." Of that particular painting the author wrote, "The hearts of the boldest painters were grieved and they hung their heads before it."

If in 1976 Arthur Houghton was auctioning off paintings from his *Shahnameh,* the Metropolitan could never own the entire book. Bound for four hundred years, its pages were being dispersed. The seriousness of this event is suggested by an article in *Art News:* "The most beautiful book in the world? Many think it is the *Shahnameh* (Book of Kings) painted by the great masters of 16th century Iran. Seeing its pages is like opening a door and seeing the Sistine ceiling for the first time."

On an impulse, I picked up my phone and called Welch at his office at Harvard. When he answered I told him of my interest in the *Shahnameh* and my dismay on reading the *Times* article. "I have not been able to sleep at night," he told me. Welch and I met for lunch a week later at La Paloma in Harvard Square. The lunch began a fascinating, albeit short, friendship. Over several more meetings he told me of his relationship with Arthur Houghton. He, too, had expected that the entire manuscript would eventually end up at the Metropolitan. He told of helping Houghton select the illustrations to give to the museum, and added, "They weren't among the best."

At some point I wrote a letter to the curator of Islamic art at the Metropolitan. I wish I had saved a copy of my letter; I do have Richard Ettinghausen's reply, dated December 16, 1976:

DEAR MR. BUFFETT:

I was away for a short while, so please forgive me if I am answering your kind letter of December 3rd only today.

It was a wonderful letter for us to receive because it shows us your genuine affection for the Islamic art and the close relationship you have been able to achieve. We have had undoubtedly many admirers of the objects which we have displayed, but never have we had amongst the many letters which we have received words of such genuine feeling as expressed in your letter to me.

Museum curators and their staff try to do their best to show the art under their care, but it is rarely that they know for sure how the public reacts. There are, of course, many visitors and they express kind compliments, but a letter like yours shows a much deeper understanding for which we are genuinely grateful.

With your kind permission, I will send the contents of the first part of your letter to Mr. Houghton, who will be delighted with it.

As to your specific questions:

1. The big publication on the Houghton Shahnameh *has been announced for many years but has not yet appeared. It will be a very large book in several volumes and as such, very expensive as it will contain many color plates and illustrations of every one of the 256 miniatures. As far as I know, no specific publication date has been announced.*

2. The "Court of Gayumarth" was included in the exhibition "A King's Book of Kings." It is illustrated in Mr. Welch's book (two color plates and one black and white plate). The miniature is still in Mr. Houghton's possession and was only a loan for the exhibition.

3. We were quite disturbed about the sale of the "Houghton" miniatures at Christie's in London on November 17, but since it is private property there is no way for us to interfere, especially since Mr. Houghton has presented to us 78 miniatures from the manuscript and has also otherwise been a benefactor to the Museum. We do not know for whom the London dealer Colnaghi bought the miniatures.

If I can be of any assistance or can provide information, I will be delighted to be at your disposal. We will always welcome you warmly in our galleries.

Sincerely yours, Richard Ettinghausen

The "big publication" referred to is Harvard University Press's two-volume facsimile edition of the *Shahnameh,* published in 1980.

The *Saturday Review of Literature* carried an article in its October 27, 1979, issue by Eleanor Munro titled "How to Mangle a Masterpiece: The Sad Story of the Houghton *Shahnameh.*" The title reveals Munro's perspective; the article adds some fascinating details. The price that Houghton is rumored to have paid for the book in 1959 is $400,000. Munro comments, "It was a sum considered outlandishly high at the time for any sort of book, but with the passing of only a few inflationary years, it would now be held unattainable for any one of its 258 parts." She reveals that when seven of its pages were auctioned off by Christie's, a single sheet went for $464,800. The article quoted one commentator as saying, "It was a great day for commerce, but hardly for the preservation of cultural treasures." According to the auction catalogue, "the manuscript is universally acknowledged as one of the supreme illustrated manuscripts of any period or culture and among the greatest works of art in the world."

When Munro asked Houghton why he had sold the pages, he replied, "What will be the eventual disposition of the large remaining number of miniatures I cannot say at this time. Of one thing I feel sure, which is that they should not all be in one place. The risks of destruction by fire, war, civil disturbance, and theft are too great. In addition, I would like to see them somewhat widely dispersed so that they can be seen and appreciated by the largest number of persons over the long future." Munro cites critics who are "outraged" and "horrified," adding, "But how are they to be seen, one wonders, unless in a public institution?"

Fortunately, I could experience at first hand what she meant. At a meeting in Welch's office, he showed me two of the paintings he had bought, both of finer quality than any that Houghton gave to the Metropolitan. I did not ask him where he'd bought them or what he'd paid. I gazed at them in wonder and awe. It was a blessing to me, but, yes, a deprivation for those who wouldn't have access to them in a museum.

Arthur Houghton died in 1992. The 120 miniatures of the *Shahnameh* still in his possession passed to his estate. This meant that between 1972 and 1992, 60 of the original 258 had been sold to private individuals or to museums. The other 78 were at the Metropolitan.

What happened to the 120 remaining miniatures? On the night of July 28, 1994, an unmarked jet carrying a painting valued at eighteen million dollars arrived at the airport in Vienna from Iran. At the same time, a van carrying nine sealed boxes arrived. The boxes contained the 120 miniatures. Under cover of darkness and without publicity, a barter took place.

Iran, anxious to reclaim part of its cultural heritage, had willingly exchanged for what remained of the *Shahnameh* a nude considered to be one of Willem de Kooning's masterpieces, *Woman III*. The painting once belonged to the shah's family but was considered decadent after the revolution and had remained hidden away. One Iranian critic called it a "savage, aggressive portrayal of a naked woman." The de Kooning was purchased in 2006 from a prior owner by the hedge fund billionaire Steven Cohen for 13.7 million dollars. The 120 miniatures, the entire text of Firdowsi's poem, and the heavy cover are currently in the Museum of Contemporary Art in Tehran.

Four years after the exchange, an article in *Art News* featured an appeal by Prince Sadruddin Aga Khan, who owned some of the *Shahnameh*'s pages. He expressed the hope that someday the entire book would be together again. One of the six paintings the prince owns is *The Court of Gayumarth*. (Welch told me one day that the prince had proposed that they jointly own the work but that he had declined, saying, "It would be like jointly owning a pair of shoes.")

Years ago, I bought a few prints from the *Shahnameh* and had them glued to poster board. I used them and slides to give a talk about the book, recounting much of what I've written here. One of the places I spoke was in the elementary school classroom in Pasadena, California, where my son Tom taught. I recall sitting on a bench after school, watching students wait for their buses. A boy from Tom's class walked up and asked for my autograph, the first time anyone had done so.

Several days before I began working on this essay an obituary appeared in the *New York Times*. It began: "Stuart Carey Welch, an internationally renowned scholar, curator and collector of Islamic and Indian art who brought many of the masterworks of these traditions to the attention of the West, died on August 13, 2008 while traveling in Hokkaido, Japan. He was 80 and lived in New Hampshire. The cause was a heart attack, his family said."

It seems fitting that I close with his words. As he wrote in the epilogue of the Harvard facsimile edition, "As we ponder these miniatures, like turning beads of a celestial rosary, we wonder if paper, pigments, and brushes were ever put to a more divine purpose." And in *A King's Book of Kings* he stated, "Above all, I express gratitude to the artists who long ago created the Houghton *Shahnameh*. When I began this study, it was to learn about art; in the end I had learned about life."

iron wall

volkswagen beetle

gold medal

pen and pad

susan kennedy

deep purple

RENEWAL

mozart horn concertos

garlic and onions

posters

night-snacking children

ames, iowa

diapers

winged life

squabbles

one-act comedy

underlings

steely-eyed

cornerstone theater

straight-backed chairs

tote bag

lie-detector tests

cool dude

ihop

pizzazz

tic-tac-toe

toaster oven

doting father

jehovah-like judgment

diet french dressing

legal seafoods

bill's biscuits

Truly over a thousand of these have come from the oven of my wood stove in Colrain. Susan's been the only one to complain, and that was only because she didn't get her fifth one. If you use butter, as I do, be sure it is cold and leave the mixture crumbly. I cut the cold butter up into little squares before processing. The aim is to leave bits of butter.

2 cups **flour**

1 tablespoon
baking powder

¼ teaspoon baking **soda**

1 teaspoon **salt**

⅓ cup (5⅓ tablespoons) cold
butter, lard, or shortening

¾ cup **buttermilk**

Preheat the oven to 450° F.

1. Mix the dry ingredients. Using a pastry blender or a food processor, cut the butter into the dry mix. Using a fork, stir in enough buttermilk to make a soft dough that leaves the sides of the bowl and sticks to the fork.

2. Knead the dough thirteen times on a lightly floured board. Roll or pat the dough until it is ¼ to ½ inch thick. Using a biscuit cutter or a small glass, cut out your biscuits and lift them onto an ungreased baking sheet, sides touching. Bake for ten to twelve minutes. They should be slightly golden on top. Serve them as quick as you can.

Miracle on Park Drive

Joel listened carefully, leaned back, looked me in the eye, and said, "You've had a miracle." I cringed. An inner voice spoke clearly: "Don't pull that stuff on me." But now, more than thirty years later, there is no word in the English language that better fits the experience I'd told him about.

I first met Joel in 1970 when I was a student at Harvard University's Graduate School of Education. A psychology professor whom I admired mentioned Joel when I asked him to recommend a psychiatrist. I called, got an appointment, and liked Joel immediately. Joel would later say, "When choosing a therapist it's important that you can hear their music and they can hear yours." I could hear Joel's music. Though his schedule was full he found time, at 7:30 in the morning, four days a week.

I was in search of a stronger sense of my masculine identity and help in my troubled marriage, but one day, after we'd been together a year, Joel commented, "We're not getting anywhere. I'm just taking your money." Regretfully, I agreed.

Why weren't we getting anywhere? Psychiatrists speak of resistance, but I prefer to think that I just wasn't ready. At that time and place, I still clung to the Bill that was. I was not yet ready for the Bill I wanted to become.

Not long afterward, my marriage ended and I retreated to a cabin in western Massachusetts. When living there was no longer sustainable

I returned to Boston and drove a cab. I was stuck, facing an iron wall, stymied, going nowhere, frustrated, sad. It was the worst of times.

With my embedded sense of failure, I called Joel and got another appointment. Every Thursday afternoon for four weeks I drove my taxi to Cambridge and met Joel in his home office. One Friday afternoon, a day after our appointment, the miracle happened.

In my blue Volkswagen Beetle, I was on Park Drive heading for Cambridge to pick up my children, Wendy and Tom. We would drive to my cabin and spend the weekend together. Just as I made the gentle turn to go under the bridge and get on Storrow Drive, I suddenly felt free of burdens that had been with me for a long time. I later pulled a phrase out of the air: "Burdens that had been with me since the third grade." That is what it felt like, and it happened suddenly. I hadn't been "working on my problems" or praying, as I'd often done in the past. After many years I felt like my real self, the person I was meant to be.

My freedom lasted the entire weekend and into the next week. It wasn't a dream or a temporary high. Life was different. A new day had arrived, and I wouldn't have exchanged it for an Oscar, a Pulitzer, or a gold medal.

The following Thursday I drove to see Joel and told him what had happened. That's when he said, "You've had a miracle." When I asked him how they happen, he said he didn't know, that he was just a witness.

Since Joel used the word, I've thought a lot about miracles. I grew up in a Protestant church and am grateful for its influence. The miracles I knew happened only in the Bible. I couldn't believe that the Lord of All the Universe would lay one on little old me at just that moment on Park Drive. A Buddhist friend said he'd read that dramatic change comes when people give up struggling. Joel was a court of last resort, a fallback, a final option when I didn't know what else to do.

What I know now is that miracles happen. How and why they do is a mystery. No explanation makes sense. Like Joel, I can't explain them, I'm only a witness.

My miracle moment grew into something I'd later tell a friend was the best thing that ever happened. I saw Joel a few more times. At one session he took a pen and pad from his side table, wrote something, and handed the paper to me. It read, "Susan Kennedy 617-642-7324."

"Call her," he said. "I think the two of you have things in common."

Six months later, Susan and I were married. Not long after that, we took Joel to dinner.

"I thought a long time and finally decided it would be a sin not to introduce the two of you to each other," Joel told us. He was traditionally trained at the Harvard Medical School. There were numerous rabbis in his family's history. What he'd done didn't come out of a textbook. It was intuitive and, for Susan and me, a triumph. We have been married for more than thirty years.

Recently Joel and I met for lunch. He's a year older than I, and as we sat down he smiled and said, "Bill, older is better." I agreed. We enjoyed a good meal together. I know Joel always carries a brief, now dog-eared, handwritten note from my mother in his billfold. He didn't need to show it to me.

It reads, "God Bless Joel."

The Joys of Divorce

Divorce doesn't begin with joy. I remember Mary's words as we left the therapist's office and walked down Harvard Street in Cambridge: "I don't think I love you anymore."

For me, there would be no joy for years.

We'd been unhappy for a long time, but divorce never entered my mind. We had two young children whom we loved, and divorce wasn't a word in my family's vocabulary. Mary laid out the plan: there would be a separation, followed by a legal separation, and then in a few weeks—thud. Divorce. We labored over details. On impossible nights, Mary took long walks or I would check into the local Y. I remember kicking something across our floor that broke an antique chest.

One weekend, Mary, the children, and I went to our cabin. A game I often played with Wendy, age eight, and Tommy, age six, was "Timber." There were plenty of dead trees in the woods; they enjoyed watching me push one down.

"TIMBER!" I shouted, shoving a barren oak.

As the tree fell, our dog came running into its path. Thinking I'd save the dog by stopping the tree's fall, I put out my right leg. The dog escaped the crash but not my thigh. Nothing broke, but in a few hours the thigh turned a deep purple, and I was limping. The injury delayed my leaving our home, but the dreaded day finally came. The children listened, then cried, and I moved to a local hotel. The year was 1972.

A lawyer helped with the details. Wendy and Tommy stayed with their mother. I kept them on Thursday nights and every other weekend. The three of us spent weekends at the cabin and Thursday nights at an apartment I'd rented in Cambridge. I made beds for them on the floor; they remember dozing off to the Mozart horn concertos.

On the weeknight they spent with me, I gave Wendy and Tom five dollars, and, while I waited in the car, they went into a supermarket and bought our dinner. We survived. On November 10, 1973, our divorce became final.

Several years later I decided on a career. Having been helped in therapy, I wanted to become a practitioner but needed a master's degree. While involved in the application process, I worked as the residence director of a psychiatric halfway house.

On May 4, 1977, my new life began.

I had a blind date arranged by a friend. Susan Kennedy and I agreed to meet at 9 P.M. at Grendel's Den in Harvard Square. I still remember her beautiful blue eyes as she looked up smiling from the bottom of the stairs. We hoped for a beer, but the Den served no liquor. We settled for tea. Having both grown up in Omaha, Nebraska, we talked about our different high schools. We spoke of our travels. We discovered that we both liked garlic and onions and agreed to spend the following Sunday together. On returning to the halfway house, I told a few residents that I'd met the woman I wanted to marry.

My former wife had been asking me to become our children's primary caretaker. I insisted I couldn't. Going back to school in my mid-forties was enough. Out of the blue, Mary called a family meeting at her place at four in the afternoon on July 1. I sat nervously in the living room of her home. The four of us gathered.

"What's up?" I asked.

Mary made a clear announcement. As of August 1 she'd no longer be the children's primary caretaker. Period. After a few more words, I asked Wendy and Tommy to get in my car. We drove to a nearby park, got out, and sat under a tree.

"I don't know how we're going to do it," I said firmly, "but, by golly, we're going to do it." Later, I'd always think of this as one of my finest moments, but today neither Wendy nor Tommy remembers it. I found an apartment near the children's schools and prepared to become a student again at Boston University's Graduate School of Social Work.

It all worked out, helped by the growing presence of Susan in our lives. She ran a preschool in a nearby suburb and brought in a steady paycheck. Wendy entered her sophomore year at Cambridge High; Tommy continued at the Agassiz Elementary School as an eighth grader, and I started classes at Boston University.

One day while Susan was visiting, Tommy asked, "Is she spending the night here?" I told him she was. Two hours later, as Susan and I were settling in, Tommy, in the adjacent bedroom, began hammering on the wall to put up posters. Another time, Wendy and Tommy were fighting loudly, as Susan and I nested in the bedroom. She said, "This is not my scene."

Fortunately, there were other scenes more to her liking. We painted the new apartment together and began to share meals. One thing she never got used to, though, was putting food in the refrigerator for lunch the next day, only to find it gone in the morning, devoured by night-snacking teenagers.

In an old diary, I found this item recalling another incident:

TUESDAY, MARCH 14, 1978.

Yesterday: Up at 4:30 a.m.—nerves; jogging at 5:45; Tom's birthday breakfast, then frosting his cake. Meeting Susan in the Square; to Harvard housing to look for an apartment; pick up Wendy at 10:50, then to Chilton Road to see an apartment, then to Porter Road and giving a $100 deposit to Mr. Gupta; to Legal Seafood for lunch with Susan; to B.U. for two hours of study; meet Tom and his four friends for an hour of bowling; home on the subway; fix fried chicken, mashed potatoes and gravy, ice cream and cake; take Tom's friends home.

THEN! *This morning I'm talking to Tom, who expresses dissatisfaction with his birthday. "Why?" I ask. "Well," he says, "I sort of expected you to drive us home from B.U."*

One afternoon, sitting under some pine trees near our cabin, I proposed to Susan. She looked into my eyes and said, "Thank you." We loved each other, but she wasn't convinced we needed to marry. We agreed, though, that if she got pregnant, we'd tie the knot.

In the same diary, I found this entry:

THURSDAY, OCTOBER 26, 1978

Last evening when Susan came home, about 6 p.m., she had an unusual look on her face and told me to come upstairs. She said she'd called Dr. Ditzion, or rather that he'd called her to say that the test results were positive. Susan is pregnant. We are going to have a baby! No one other than Joel knows yet.

We were married in Ames, Iowa, by Susan's uncle Carl, a Lutheran pastor. Tommy, dressed in white, led the wedding procession carrying a candle. Eight months later, on June 27, 1979, at 2:59 A.M., baby Noah arrived. We found a larger apartment. Wendy and Tommy learned to change diapers. I dusted off old skills, made new by Noah and Susan.

For years *The Joy of Cooking* has been a best-seller. *The Joy of Sex* was one, too. Amazon lists many "joy" books, including *The Joys of Chemistry* and even *The Joy of Rhubarb*. The authors aren't dumb. Joy sells.

In my experience, divorce brings no joy, but it can eventually lead to a better life. In the midst of divorce, my glass was empty. Down the road, the glass began to fill, and, in fleeting moments, overflow.

Cooking, sex, chemistry, and rhubarb aren't really filled with joy. Each can bring moments of happiness, excitement, satisfaction, and wonder, but the joy is fleeting, as William Blake wrote:

> He who binds to himself a joy
> Doth the winged life destroy,
> But he who kisses the joy as it flies
> Lives in Eternity's sunrise.

More than one hundred thousand books in print have "Divorce" in the title. There is even one called *Divorce for Dummies*. But for each person who gets divorced, the process is unique. I once made the mistake of telling a fellow whose wife had asked for a divorce to hang in there, that it took me five years to find a new life. That was my experience, but it wouldn't necessarily be his.

Pain, and plenty of it, is the common thread, but the thread from which something new can be created. While driving a taxi, I had no dream or hope of ever being married again, of having another child, of coming into a new life.

But I did, and it was made possible by divorce.

Susan, Noah, Wendy, and Tommy. Therein lies the joy.

west indian chicken, peas, and rice

During the 1990s I was on the board of *Spare Change,* a newspaper sold in the Boston area by homeless men and women. I got an idea. I decided to interview local chefs and obtain recipes for people with limited income. These were published in the paper. My friend Linda Larson gave the column the name "Daily Bread." Here is the recipe from Arlene Romney, the chef de cuisine at the restaurant at Boston's Museum of Fine Arts.

1–2 tablespoons vegetable oil
1 large white onion, diced
1 carrot, peeled and diced small
4 cloves garlic, minced
2 lbs. chicken breast, diced
2½ cups Uncle Ben's Rice
1 can (28 oz.) pigeon peas
1 jalapeño pepper, seeds removed, diced
1½ cups coconut milk
Enough water or stock to cover the rice
½ stick butter, cut into small pieces
½ bunch parsley
Salt and pepper to taste

1. Heat the oil in the bottom of a Dutch oven and sauté the onion and carrot until soft. Add the garlic and cook a minute more.

2. Add the chicken and sauté until the chicken has lost its color, about 3 minutes.

3. Add the rice, peas, jalapeño, coconut milk, salt and pepper to taste. Stir. Add enough stock or water to cover the rice. Cover and simmer for 30 minutes. Stir in the butter and parsley. Taste. Adjust seasoning and serve.

Chef Romney added: "Pigeon peas are small peas. Your favorite bean or frozen peas may be used. Another fresh herb, such as oregano, thyme, or chives, can be substituted for the parsley or in addition to it."

Sganarelle

After receiving a graduate degree in social work, I was hired as the first director of a newly created unit inside a state mental hospital in Boston. We held a contest to give the unit a name. Lots of ordinary names were submitted, and if you weren't mentally ill, two funny ones: Chock-Full-O-Nuts and The Schiz-Carleton. The winner was The Fenwood Inn, named for the hospital's address, 74 Fenwood Road.

The Inn was for people who didn't need to be locked up. Our doors opened at 4 P.M. on weekdays and closed the next morning at 8 A.M. They remained open around the clock on weekends and holidays. The Inn's residents still needed a protected environment. The goal was that they'd eventually move to a halfway house in the community. On weekdays they received treatment—various group therapies—in a day hospital adjacent to the Inn. Residents returned to the Inn at the end of the day.

I worked with fifteen mental health workers (MHWs) who were there to assign beds, settle squabbles, hand out toothpaste, play games, and do a variety of things to keep a fifty-bed unit in a semblance of order.

As the director of a nonmedical unit, I could introduce a number of experiences not common in the treatment of the mentally ill. One of the best was a genuine theatrical production. An MHW named Holly Samuels, a recent Harvard graduate, told me about a classmate of hers named Bill Rauch who was interested in theater. He was looking for a group to work with; he wanted to produce a play.

Bill and I met, got acquainted, and talked over a few details. He was an energetic and creative presence with a smiling round face. Over the course of several months, he showed up one or two evenings per week, first to select and then to rehearse the cast, all of whom were Inn residents. Margaret, Ricky, Doris, Willie, Matthew, and Scott were among the cast members. Bill chose a one-act comedy by Molière called *Sganarelle*.

One morning I came to work and read the Inn's log, a chronicle of events from the night staff. I saw this note from Holly:

A note about theater group last night: Bill Rauch was rehearsing Margaret M. and Willie C. in a difficult scene from the middle of the play. Bill, in a very non-threatening way, was offering suggestions, in a word, directing the play. But Margaret became increasingly defensive and, concomitantly, more delusional. She started referring to "the underlings" who "don't understand anything." At this point, I would have backed down for fear that Margaret would escalate even further and lose control. Bill, however, kept going. He's the director and he had a point to make, hence Margaret had to listen. Much to my surprise and relief, Margaret kept it together.

I am very ambivalent about this episode. On one hand, I think Bill's response may have been unsafe. On the other, his refusal to pander to her delusions may have forced her to behave like a "not crazy" human being. It was good to see how an outsider, with much higher expectations than I, helped Margaret rise to the occasion.

A dress rehearsal and three performances were scheduled to take place in the courtyard, a grass picnic area surrounded by hospital buildings. The day of the dress rehearsal came. A light rain was falling and two cast members were in the Intensive Care Unit, a locked unit for those who were "decompensating," possibly becoming psychotic. The rehearsal was moved to the gym. When I went in, several of the housekeeping staff were there, moving some tables around. I asked them to stop, saying that we had a performance in thirty minutes. Up on the I.C.U., I found one of the cast members was well enough to be out for an hour. He joined the group.

The rehearsal went well, a friend of Bill's filling in for the missing cast member. Two in the cast had minor roles—my son Noah and his buddy Jeremy, ages seven and eight. Twice during the play they rode their bikes across the stage to provide local color.

That Thursday I had to go out of town for the weekend. When I returned Monday morning, I learned that again because of rain, Thursday's and Friday's performances had been in the gym. Saturday night Holly wrote the following note in the log:

The last night of the play was performed, finally, out in the courtyard with a proper set. A lovely finale to a very worthwhile project. I think the most important thing about Sganarelle *was that it gave the participants something of which they could be proud. As Rick, Margaret, Betty, Jim, Matt, and Willie passed among their "fans" they positively glowed. It was their night—well earned, well deserved. . . . It is too rare that we have a night like this on the Inn: energetic, productive, cohesive, and fun. A real treat.*

That same Monday I was reprimanded by the hospital's business manager, John Gibbs, a porcine, steely-eyed, and, to use the local lingo, anal-retentive man. "Buffett," he said, "on Thursday you prevented my men from moving tables in the gym. Don't you ever do that again."

Several weeks later Bill Rauch and I sat down to coffee. We had a good time reprising the experience. Rauch commented, "You know, Bill, we had so many problems that at times I wondered if we'd be able to pull it off." After a thoughtful pause he added, "But if I had a theater and somebody tried to put a mental hospital inside, boy, I'd really have a problem with that!"

A local elementary school became Bill's next venture in community theater, followed by his buying a van with some friends and traveling to small towns across America. Once settled, they would introduce themselves to townsfolk and begin involving them in a theatrical production—publicity, selling tickets, assembling costumes, building sets, and, of course, acting. They called their effort "The Cornerstone Theater Company" and were eventually publicized in various national media. In one small southern town they put on a production of *Romeo and Juliet* that attracted the attention of *American Theater* magazine. Pictured on its cover were the two leads, an African-American male and a white female.

Years passed, and the company eventually settled in Los Angeles. Cornerstone never ceased to be innovative, sometimes blending different ethnic groups in their casts, and once, as they did on the Inn, involving patients, this time those from an AIDS hospice.

A few years ago, Bill was named director of the Shakespeare Festival in Ashland, Oregon. Before he left Cornerstone, the company held several receptions around the country for him to say goodbye and to introduce the new director. Along with about fifty others, I attended one in New York City. During the evening, Bill said some appreciative words to a few people. He thanked me, saying that the Massachusetts Mental Health Center on a unit for the chronically mentally ill is "where it all began."

Bernadette Conducts

When I was director of the Fenwood Inn, I wanted to offer residents informal evening and weekend programs that would help expand their world beyond the traditional therapies offered in mental hospitals. I wanted to bring in the arts and other programs to bring about fresh perspectives. Sometimes, I discovered, I was the one whose perspective shifted.

I had heard of an organization in New York City called Art Reach, which brought performers of various kinds into institutional settings around the city. I adopted the idea for the Inn. One of my first contacts was the New England Conservatory of Music, specifically its honors groups. Only outstanding students were admitted to these ensembles. In return for being selected, they gave several community concerts.

I called the young woman who directed the program, and we agreed that different groups would perform at the Inn several times per year. The concerts were held in a room called "the chapel," a nicely appointed place with straight-backed chairs and a modest carpet. It hosted a Catholic Mass on Sundays, departmental staff meetings, seminars, and events like my Art Reach program.

One of the first honors groups was a string quartet. On the night of the concert, an Inn resident named Bernadette arrived thirty minutes early. For a while, only the two of us were in the chapel. Bernadette wore baggy clothes and carried a tote bag from a Caribbean resort. Her diagnosis was chronic schizophrenia, but her symptoms were significantly modified by medication. She settled herself in the center of the second row and began sorting through items in her bag.

The musicians arrived and the seats began to fill with patients/concertgoers. No one sat next to Bernadette. At eight the concert began. I stood by the door to greet late arrivals and encourage them to enter quietly, but my attention soon focused on Bernadette. As the musicians played, she started to conduct. Her gestures were grand, sweeping, constant, and seen by all.

I cringed and clenched my jaw. Inside, I was steaming with Jehovah-like judgment and wanted to remove her, get her out of there. But the concert went on and everyone else seemed to enjoy it.

As people filed out, I walked back to where the honors program coordinator was sitting. Before I could apologize for Bernadette, she beamed and said how well everything had gone. "Did you see that woman in the front conducting the music?" she asked. "Wasn't it wonderful?" She added that at some of their gatherings people fall asleep—but not here at the Inn, at least not Bernadette.

I kept my thoughts to myself, realizing that what had been a growing annoyance to me had provided utter joy to the musicians. Now, before rushing to judgment, I try to remember Bernadette and the night she conducted the string quartet.

strawberry shortcake

Of the several strawberry shortcake recipes I've tried, this is the best. It comes from Pam Anderson's *The Perfect Recipe.* With it and a little effort you can pass by the plastic wrapped pieces of angel food cake usually found next to fresh strawberries in the supermarket. There are three components: the strawberries, the shortcakes, and the whipped cream.

3 pints strawberries

6 tablespoons sugar

2 cups flour

½ teaspoon salt

1 tablespoon baking powder

5 tablespoons sugar, divided

1 stick unsalted butter, frozen

1 large egg, beaten

1 egg white, lightly beaten

½ cup half-and-half

½ pint heavy cream

1 tablespoon sugar

strawberries:

Wash and pare the strawberries. Crush 2 pints with a potato masher and quarter the other pint. Combine and add 6 tablespoons of sugar.

shortcakes:

1. Adjust the oven rack to the lower-middle position and preheat to 425°.

2. Mix the flour, salt, baking powder, and 3 tablespoons of the sugar in a medium bowl. Grate the butter into the dry ingredients. Toss to coat. Use a pastry cutter to finish cutting in the butter. Butter pieces should be the size of split peas.

3. Mix the whole egg with the half-and-half and pour into the flour mixture. Mix with a fork until the dough starts to form a ball and come away from the sides of the bowl. Turn the dough onto a floured board, gather it together, and lightly knead it.

4. Pat the dough into a ¾-inch-thick round. Dip a biscuit cutter in flour—I use the rim of a small glass—and make as many rounds as possible. Place them an inch apart on an ungreased baking sheet. Brush the tops with the egg white and sprinkle them with the remaining 2 tablespoons of sugar. Bake 12 to 14 minutes until golden brown. Cool on a wire rack until warm.

whipped cream:

Whip one cup of chilled heavy cream to soft peaks with 1 tablespoon of sugar.

assembly:

Cut each shortcake in half. Spoon some berries over the bottom half and place in a bowl. Put on the top. Add more berries and some whipped cream.

If you like, you can beat a little more sugar and a teaspoon of vanilla into the whipped cream.

Serves six.

Stranglehold

Someone tried to strangle me once. I could tell immediately that the attack wasn't meant to be lethal. The fingers never tightened around my neck.

The day began as a typical Friday. I sat in my office at the Fenwood Inn, part of Mass Mental, which operated a state facility to treat people with mental illness. I had arrived early that morning for my weekly meeting with the night staff. Their shift had started at midnight and would end at 8 A.M., when all the residents were up, dressed, and on their way to breakfast. Our meeting over, I'd gone to my office, closed the door, and sat down to do some paperwork while the night staff attended to the residents.

Suddenly, the door opened. Someone came up from behind. The hands weren't those of a patient, but those of Alex Jackson, a member of the night staff. When I jumped up to break his hold, he ran out. He said later that he'd come in to talk and I'd attacked him. There were no witnesses. There'd been no noise.

I called Security, which arrived a few minutes later, along with Paul Riccardi, Mass Mental's assistant superintendent. Paul told me to go down to Southard Clinic, the outpatient clinic, and be evaluated by the doctor on call. Fortunately, Dr. Bill Boucher was on duty that morning. Bill was an old hand at state service and at mental illness. Included in his report were the words "light abrasion marks on the right and left side of neck." I will never know if he really saw them or if he just knew what might be helpful in the days ahead.

The union supported Alex. Paul offered lie detector tests to both of us, which Alex refused. I passed mine. Several times Paul expressed surprise that Alex would assault me "after what you did for him when he was jailed."

The jailing had occurred many months earlier when I got a call at home in the early hours of the morning. Alex had been arrested. There'd been a robbery in the hospital neighborhood, and Alex, on a break from work, was being held as a suspect. At dawn I went to the courthouse, saw him in his cell, and later, testified as a character witness. The Alex I knew was law-abiding and on the quiet side.

The judge released him. Justice prevailed. The incident was my first experience with "racial profiling," in which black men in America become suspects only because they're black.

I would describe Alex as a smart, wiry African-American, on the short side, who had been on the Mass Mental staff when I arrived several years earlier. He wore glasses, had a goatee, presented himself as a cool dude, and had a wry, often sarcastic sense of humor. His job was far beneath his capabilities.

But that morning in my office, Alex betrayed his mild manner. In the weeks that followed, the wheels of justice turned slowly. Alex was off work until a decision was made. His appeals were denied. The final step occurred one morning downtown in a state office. Alex, with his union representative, and I with Paul Riccardi, met with the hearing officer, whose decision would be final.

The hearing ended in our favor. Boucher's report determined the outcome. The hearing officer noted that the union never questioned the doctor's finding of "light abrasion marks on the right and left side of neck." Alex never returned to work and, at last report, had headed for California. I returned to my job, none the wiser.

Why did Alex do it? I can only guess. I'm white and was his boss. He had a dead-end job and felt frustration. Alex often worked a double shift; perhaps he had done so that morning and was tired. Alex alone knows why—and he never talked. Even now, all these years later, I can only wonder, as so many of us do, when silence is the only response we get.

Breakfast With Tom

Long ago, the IHOP near Fresh Pond Circle in Cambridge, Massachusetts, yielded to a gas station, but my memory of a breakfast I had there twenty years ago with my son Tom remains clear. I'm sure we had pancakes, but more memorable was our conversation.

At the time, I wasn't worried about Tom. Twenty-five, single, and living on the West Coast, he was gainfully employed in the field of education. The time for raising him had passed long ago, but I must have thought I still had wisdom to impart.

Tom's mother and I had divorced years earlier, and there'd been some difficult times. I lived alone in a one-room basement apartment not far from the garage of Checker Taxi, for which I drove a cab. Mired in a meager and diminished life, I felt that the road ahead was closed. Though I never thought seriously of suicide, I imagined a button at the base of my thumb. If pressed, I would disappear. I pressed it often.

But by the morning of our breakfast, life had changed dramatically. I'd remarried, had another child, and found a good job. I was forty-six.

Reflecting on my old life over breakfast, I told Tom, "Today, I look at driving a taxi differently. Back then it was the worst time in my life. Today, I'm glad to have been a cab driver; I recall the experience with gratitude. Telling people I drove a taxi adds pizzazz to my life story. I can point a prideful thumb at my chest and say, 'Hey, I was a cab driver.'"

Clearly I had Tom's ear. I continued, emphasizing that what seems barren and devoid of purpose at one time can much later become a plus—something that adds richness and vitality to one's history. I expected him to look up admiringly and say something like, "Wow, Dad, what a great story." Instead he asked, "You know what's been like that in my life?" Fortunately, I kept my mouth shut. What ran through my head was: Oh, son, there's been nothing like that in your young life. I asked, "No, what?"

Tom looked me in the eye and replied, "My struggles with you."

What? I thought. Struggles with me? To me, his adolescence had been something I'd moved through and left behind, but he remembered our difficulties. Later he realized that these struggles had been useful. What was once tough came to seem valuable later.

I do remember his coming to me when he was a freshman in high school and asking if he could get an apartment with friends for the coming summer. I gave him a firm no but agreed to think about it. A week later he made the same request. Again: no. He responded, "Well, what'll you do if I just walk out of here? You can't stop me." I responded, "I'll call the police."

That quieted him down. Little did I know that I'd look back on the moment as my last hurrah. Late one afternoon a year later, we came home from a weekend at our cabin, the car full of stuff. I wanted help carrying it in, but Tom went into the bathroom and locked the door. I did a slow burn and yelled a few times. Eventually he came out of the bathroom and stopped a few inches from my face. I don't remember our words but I'll never forget my thought: he could deck me if he wanted. Our relationship had changed. He who had been "Tommy" was now "Tom."

In an old journal I found more evidence of some of our clashes. At that point Tom, Wendy, Susan, and I were living together. Tom had started high school. I'd found a therapist for him and insisted that he go. His mother, now remarried, planned to move to California. On February 22, 1978, I wrote:

I'm still in the after-effects of Tom's outburst on Monday night.

"I don't want to live with you."

"I can't stand Stuart [the therapist] *and you're a jerk for wasting money on him."*

"You expect me to be perfect."

"I feel crummy around you, but really good until I get home."

These were repeated themes. And that night he put into the hallway things I had given him—a pair of boots, a bottle of diet French dressing, some baseball books, bed sheets, a pair of Levi's. He came into my room and took back his gifts of a boat and a tic-tac-toe game. His attack was a blow. Two days later I wrote:

I've been thinking about Tom's outburst on Monday. Two points:

He'd asked how long he had to live with me. "I'm not going to stay around that long. Do I have any choice about where I live? Boy, that doesn't sound like a choice to me."

"Will you give me $1.50 so I can buy a lock for my door?"

I believe these are control issues. Tom's feeling a lack of control over his life and is trying to get some. Putting my gifts to him in the hallway and taking back his gifts to me reflects an effort to separate, to define himself as a distinct person.

As I later found value in having driven a taxi, so Tom eventually found value in his difficulties with me.

When I was writing this, I asked Tom what we'd fought about so many years ago. He couldn't recall many specifics, but he did remember something about the toaster oven. Apparently I'd told him he wouldn't be able to use it unless he got home on time at night. He admitted I'd only been half-serious but he added, "It was something that cemented my desire to become independent from you."

An adage I coined when my children were growing up was, "If I win, I lose. If I lose, I win." I exaggerate for the sake of emphasis. What I really meant was that if I win every struggle with my children, they'll grow up dependent, feeling cowed, and not knowing their own minds. If I lose, both of us will win. They'll grow up independent and self-willed.

Today Tom is married and has two very young daughters. He has a doctorate from the Harvard School of Education and is on the staff at Michigan State University. We visit Tom's family as often as we can, and it is clear he is a doting father and a good husband. Our relationship is mutually supportive, easy, and loving. Small as it may seem, I'm happy that he has four pictures of me on his refrigerator and that he often puts his arm around me. He could still deck me, but the urge has passed.

baolian's noodle soup

It has been a many-faceted blessing to have Baolian Qin in our family. Chinese food is but one. On Chinese New Year I joined six others in Tom and Baolian's kitchen and made probably three hundred Chinese dumplings. I wasn't in a Chinese village where the activity is a communal affair, but most of my companions were Chinese, and I was doing something my grandmother never did on her Nebraska farm.

When I asked Baolian for her noodle soup recipe, she wrote it out on a piece of paper.

1. Boil a large pot of water (you can always start with chicken broth, which will give more flavor).

2. Mix ground pork with some minced ginger, scallion, soy sauce, a little cornstarch, and, if needed, a little water. Beat in one direction for one minute.

3. After the water boils, use a spoon and put some ground pork mixture into your palm. Make little balls, about the size of ping-pong balls, and put into the water.

4. After the soup boils again, add some chopped tofu and mushrooms.

5. Put in the noodles (not too many; noodles soak up water easily).

6. Try the noodles after 4 minutes or so. If they are ready you can take the noodles out of the pot.

7. Put any vegetable you like into the soup, for example, bok choy, spinach, kale—make sure there is enough liquid in the soup after it boils again. Salt to taste, then pour soup over the noodles.

Notes:

As you can see, Baolian's guidelines don't specify the amount of each ingredient. The basic message is that this recipe is very flexible. For those who want specifics, I add the following notes (numbered to correspond with Baolian's directions):

1. You can use half water and half chicken broth. Some Asian food stores sell specially flavored chicken broth. I've never used it, but Baolian does.

2. For the meatballs you can use ½ to 1 pound of ground pork; perhaps a 1-inch piece of fresh ginger, peeled and diced; a bunch of scallions (white and semi-green parts) cut in ¼-inch pieces; 2 tablespoons soy sauce; and 2 teaspoons cornstarch.

4. Use 7 to 14 ounces of chopped firm tofu and one or two cups of chopped mushrooms.

5. Baolian gave me an ample supply of "Wu-Mu Dry Noodles" in a box. These are flat, about a foot long, and ⅛ inch wide. Look for them in an Asian market. I don't recommend rice noodles or regular ones made for the American market; however, the soup won't explode if you use them.

6. You can cook the noodles seperately in water or in the soup. If you cook them in the soup, add more chicken broth, probably three quarts instead of two.

7. If you use kale, cut the leaves from the stalk and chop them up. I like to use bok choy because it is Chinese. I take a head and slice it thinly.

Please remember that this recipe is very flexible, depending on how many you want to serve and what you like. The above recipe serves four people.

Ping-Pong Partner

Life has its coincidences, and I've had my share. One stands out. Years ago my wife and I went to dinner at Legal Seafoods in Cambridge. Back then diners sat together at long tables. We sat across from each other at the end of one of them. Soon two other couples were seated beside us. One of the women sat next to me.

We exchanged a few words. Both couples were tourists from the South. When I commented on the woman's lack of an accent, she said she'd grown up in Minnesota. I told her that I'd gone to school in Minnesota and mentioned my alma mater, Carleton College. She nodded. I continued, "My family used to vacation in Minnesota, north of the Twin Cities, near Fergus Falls."

"Where?" she asked.

"At a place called Dunvilla."

"What's your name?"

"Bill Buffett."

Her jaw dropped. "We used to play ping-pong! I'm Virginia Dunn!"

rabbit, rabbit

hard rock café

mickey mantle   forest hills   martin luther king

lib

sandlot football   gandhi

light-fingered fellow   scraggly tree   rutted road

arroyos   bear skeleton

two tons of silver   world trade center

salvation army

willa cather   homecoming   improbable consequences

spears and shields

tortured love

INTO

MY

OWN

sloppy soccer

legos   tail lights   swath of cotton

southern hemisphere

proboscidea

guaranteed grade

electrocution

district 9   cornhuskers   old maid

chivas on the rocks   taproot

tool shed

uncle wiggly   fireflies in a jar   newborn calf   may queen gown

dusty and bumpy

penn station

paul bunyan   big apple   grand tier

house salad   kibitzing

decca records

a few mints   damn the torpedoes

revival meetings

gooey nut sauce

bean sprouts

willa salute

stepladder

a cuddle   walt whitman   wrinkled

kick butt

ovarian lottery

buttons and bows

milky way galaxy

Ben, My Friend

The phone rang. I answered it.

"Mr. Buffett. This is Ben."

I knew the voice and remembered why he was calling. Of course. It was late afternoon on the last day of the month, August 31, 2008. He often calls on the last day of the month.

"I'm calling to remind you of what to say seven hours and twenty-two minutes from now."

I knew: "Rabbit, rabbit." In Ben's world, if these were my first words after midnight, I'd have a month's worth of good luck.

Ben is my most unusual friend. He remembers the exact date in 1983 when we first met. I spotted him from my front yard, sitting forlornly under the big tree in front of his house. Ben, his mother, his sister, and his step-dad had just moved in across the street. I walked over to ask what was bothering him. "My dad drove up Monadnock Street," he said, "and I wanted to come up Academy Road." I learned that Ben's dad lived in a nearby town and had brought Ben home after a visit.

A few years passed. On a Saturday afternoon, Ben and his mother Cheryl, my wife and I, and a neighbor walked into Boston's Hard Rock Café. The outing was Ben's idea. Inside, rock music competed with the sounds of voices and clanging plates. We sat down and looked at menus. When the waiter who came to take our drink order reeled off the possibilities—orange, Coke, 7-Up, and root beer—Ben said, "I'd like a glass of all of them mixed together." The waiter didn't blink.

For every musical selection we heard, Ben could name the artist, title, label, and the year it was recorded. The guy had a unique ability and enjoyed showing it off.

Another of his talents was being able to give the day of the week for any date and year. Ben is the only fellow I know who can tell me that the day I was born, January 27, 1933, fell on a Friday. That afternoon I asked him to do the same for my wife and the neighbor who'd come with us. Ben proudly obliged.

After eating, as we were getting ready to leave, Cheryl penned a note to leave with the tip: "Thank you for being so nice to my son." And she made a gentle request of me, one I've never forgotten. It concerned asking Ben the day of the week for any date. She hoped I wouldn't do it: "I prefer that my son not be considered a freak."

Ben has a label: autistic. I hesitate to mention it. Labels tell such partial truths. Identifying George Bush as a Republican leaves a lot out. It's the same with simply identifying Mickey Mantle a Yankee.

So it is with Ben. Calling him "autistic" leaves out a whole lot.

A year after the Hard Rock lunch, Ben wanted to go on another neighborhood outing. I was the only one up for it. That was the beginning. Since 1992, when Ben was fifteen and I hit fifty-nine, we've had two outings a year. For me, the journey from thinking of Ben as handicapped to considering him my friend took several years.

In the beginning, when Ben called I'd feel annoyed. He would want to set a date, then call later to tell me the route he wanted to take, the movie he wanted to see, and the place we'd have lunch. It was a standard routine. I'd be rather peeved because I couldn't think about bus routes several months ahead and didn't really care. But Ben has a thing about Boston's public transportation system. He knows the routes he's never taken but intends to, and he knows which ones he has taken in only one direction. He needs to take those the other way, to achieve some sort of wholeness. Selecting the route is a sacred task. He'd tell me: "We'll drive to Forest Hills and get on Bus #45 to Copley, then from Copley get on the Green Line to Lechmere, then take #61 to Harvard Square. We could eat at Bertucci's, then go to *Dumb and Dumber*, at the Harvard Square Theater. Then we get on bus #84 to Dudley, and take the #21 back to Forest Hills." Sometimes we negotiate because the route he proposes is too long, but for the most part, I don't mind, and his way becomes our way. Ben always orders clam chowder for lunch. If the movie doesn't appeal to me, I read in the lobby.

After living across the street from me, Ben moved with his family to Memphis, then to Washington, D.C. He comes up twice a year to visit his father, and that's when we schedule our outings. He now lives, with some supervision, in his own apartment. He shaves and has a cell phone. He spends most of his time traveling on Washington's subway system and going to movies.

Who is Ben? Shortly after our outings began, we were driving toward a parking lot near our first bus station when he asked, "So who's going to take me on these outings after you're dead? You're getting pretty old, you know." I chuckled. One thing I like about Ben is that I'll hear things I hear from no one else and go places I'd never go by myself.

Here's another memorable comment. We had boarded the subway in Boston, and I'd sat next to a young African-American male. Ben was on my other side. In a very audible voice he said, "Aren't you glad they shot Martin Luther King?"

I winced mightily. Our stop couldn't come soon enough. Out on the platform I pleaded, "Why, Ben, did you make that comment about Martin Luther King?"

"Because," he explained, "since they shot him, blacks and whites can sit together on the subway."

Ben has certain rituals and takes medicine to help keep them under control. If the two us are walking along the sidewalk, he'll stop to touch a fire hydrant, a store window, the pavement, a vending machine. Sitting beside me as I drive, he'll reach over to touch the dashboard or down to touch the floor mat. He makes odd sounds. I once asked him, "Ben, why do you do these things?"

In a sheepish voice, he said, "I don't know."

One of his common rituals is sitting in a Boston subway car and loudly announcing, "Next stop: Back Bay, I think," then "Next stop Kenmore Square, I think." And on he would go, announcing each stop for the rest of the route. People would look at him, being sure to keep their distance. When I asked Ben why he did this, he told me about a movie he'd seen in which Ray Charles plays a blind bus driver who announces: "Next stop, Elm St., I think."

One day I'd had enough and told him to move to the far end of the car if he wanted to continue. He sat beside me quietly for about a minute before opting to move. Soon the announcements began from the other end of the car. "Next stop: Central Square, I think."

At the end of an outing, Ben often asks if he can give me a hug.

I remember going across the street one day after the family had just returned from vacation. I walked into the house but saw only Mike, Ben's stepfather, sitting in the front room. I called, "Ben?" I heard his voice from upstairs. Mike was thumbing through the mail and everybody was trying to settle back in, so I didn't stay. As I turned to leave, I said, "It's so good to hear Ben's voice again."

"Buffett," Mike said, "you're like the white social worker who comes into the slums during the day and returns to your warm home at night."

I've always appreciated Mike's honesty. Life with Ben 24/7 could not be easy.

Not long ago Ben began calling me "Llib." I let it go for a while but finally asked him why.

"Well, I like you a lot but I don't like your name."

I like both Ben and his name. There'll be no "Neb" for me.

A few years ago, I said to him, "Ben, you've decided where and how we'd go on our outings. Well, now it's my turn. I get to decide."

Our outings are less strenuous now. We go to Harvard Square for lunch. I then go to a movie, while Ben rides around on public transportation. We meet up afterwards. It's worked very well.

A while ago Ben called. I'd gone to bed, but this time he wanted to talk to my wife. The next day, she gave me his message:

"I don't want to be impolite or say bad things, Sue, but Bill is seventy-five, and my grandmother died when she was 76. Will you do special things with me when he's dead?"

Ben, my friend.

greek salad

I've made this salad many times, for friends' events and our traditional Easter dinner, and never tire of it. Our friend Doug Koch asked if I could make it for the gathering after his funeral, a request I will try to honor although Doug is a good ten years younger than I.

The salad has three advantages: it's reasonably healthy, it's easy, and it looks impressive. Buy firm iceberg lettuce—I learned at my father's grocery store that the heads should be hard and not soft.

salad:

2 large, solid heads of iceberg lettuce

3 green peppers, sliced

2 large red onions, thinly sliced

5 small or pickling cucumbers, sliced

3 bunches radishes, cleaned and sliced

12 plum tomatoes

2 large blocks feta cheese

(approximately 1½ lbs. total)

2 pints Kalamata olives

1 jar pepperoncini

dried organo and thyme to taste

Cut the lettuce into chunks and place them as close together as possible on a large platter. Next put a layer of sliced green pepper, followed by a layer of sliced red onion. Add the sliced cucumbers followed by the sliced radishes, and then the tomatoes. I cut these in quarters, and then cut each quarter in half.

Once all this is in place, crumble the feta and sprinkle it over the top, then sprinkle the olives and pepperoncini all around. Finally, sprinkle a bit of dried oregano or thyme lightly over the top.

dressing:

Use a jar with a lid. Pour in 3 parts olive oil to 1 part wine vinegar. Chop about 3 cloves of garlic and add a tablespoon of Dijon mustard. Add a pinch of sugar, ample salt, and fresh ground pepper. Shake and refrigerate. Pour the dressing over it just before serving.

These are the fundamentals. All else depends on your tastes.

"My Hero!"

I had lived for seventy-two years and never been in a fight. When I was in high school and attending YMCA summer camp, Fritz Adams used to come up and hit me on both arms. I went home with black and blue marks and told people I'd been hit by oars. I wasn't a sissy; I played sandlot football with the guys and basketball in a back alley, but I was scared to fight.

I once told my football-playing son that never having been in a real roll-in-the-dirt fight had left me feeling deficient. I'd missed a life experience. His response—"Gosh, dad, you're just like Gandhi"—made me feel better.

But the momentous day came in 2005. On vacation in Paris, my wife and I were emerging one hot afternoon from the Chatalet Metro station. We were looking forward to closing the door of our hotel room and resting. Just before we reached the station exit's top step, I glanced over and saw a young, light-fingered fellow pawing through my wife's backpack. With my left hand clenched and all the force I could muster, I swung my fist up and straight into his jaw. He let out a cry of pain. His left hand moved to a breast pocket in his coat, and for a second I thought he was going to draw a knife. He didn't. As I shouted, "Thief! Thief! Thief!" he turned and disappeared down the subway stairs.

After expressing her relief, my wife looked at me and said, "My hero."

Wow, I thought. Though the incident wasn't a fight, I had finally, in anger, hit someone. Take that, Fritz Adams.

As Vultures Circled

In the middle of nowhere on a hot Mexican afternoon, I had just crawled under a bush to escape the sun and had no intention of moving. But the sight of three vultures circling overhead changed my mind. I wasn't worried, but knew I couldn't relax. We'd seen the vultures earlier that day as our van bumped along a rutted dirt road. Off to the right and down in a ravine they were feasting on the body of a dead horse. We knew we weren't in Kansas anymore.

The previous day, I had flown from Boston to Guadalajara and taken a local bus west to the town of Tecolotlan. The rendezvous point for my group was the Hotel Plaza, a one-star hotel definitely unrelated to its namesake in New York City.

As part of Earthwatch, a worldwide sponsor of scientific explorations, our group of seven would be helping Dr. Oscar Carranza, a paleontologist from the University of Mexico, with his research. Our job on this trip: prospecting for fossils in the Sierra Madre Mountains.

For several years Dr. C.'s goal has been to document what some call the Great American Interchange. Several million years ago, North and South America were separate continents until a land bridge—now the Isthmus of Panama—rose up and joined the two bodies of land. Animals of all sorts, heretofore confined to either continent, were free to roam south or north. We were to help Dr. C. document this migration.

After a simple breakfast at the hotel each morning, we climbed in a van and drove into the countryside. We'd turn up dirt roads and finally stop at places Dr. C. knew. The landscape was barren except for some bushes and an occasional scraggly tree. We traversed flatlands and arroyos (gullies made by intermittent streams). Annual spring rains washed down the arroyos carrying soil and, we hoped, revealing bits of fossil.

We were not uncovering skeletons of dinosaurs, which roamed the earth more than two hundred million years ago. The land bridge connecting North and South America formed only about three million years ago. The remains we found, often quite small, once belonged to horses, camels, mice, cougars, bears, porcupines, and many more species. We hunted with our heads down. Often I'd bring something to Dr. C. only to have him shake his head and inform me that what I held was stone, not bone.

Occasionally one of us found something of special interest. The item would be carefully removed and taken back to the parking lot of the hotel, where it would be wrapped in wet plaster, a process called "jacketing." One evening at dinner I asked Dr. C. what his dream find would be, and he said, "A complete skeleton of a bear."

The majority of living beings leave no trace when they die. It is truly a matter of dust to dust. I asked a friend of mine named Greg, who owns a car service and regularly drives the eminent Harvard evolutionary biologist E. O. Wilson, to get some information for me. "Ask him this," I said. "Of everything that ever lived, how many became fossils?"

"Less than one in 1,000,000," Wilson told Greg.

"And of those," Greg asked, "how many have been found?"

Wilson estimated, "Of those one in a million that have left a trace, about one in a million of them."

Put simply, relatively very few fossils have been found and preserved. One discovery involved my parents. One summer many decades ago, my parents were down on the Nebraska farm where my mother was born. They were heading to Inavale, a small town nearby. Just before the Inavale Bridge, in a dirt embankment to the left, they noticed something white. They got out to take a closer look, wondering if it was a bone. They notified a high school chum of my mother's, Bertrand Schultz, who happened to be the director of the natural history museum at the university.

I heard nothing more, but when I inquired recently at the museum, I received the following reply:

The fossils in question come from the Lawrence McCall farm just south of Inavale near the Inavale Bridge. Fred and Katherine Buffett notified Bertrand Schultz, director of the museum, of these bones in late November 1945. Lloyd Tanner and Bob Kubicek of the museum visited the site on June 1, 1946 and returned on June 28–30 to do some excavating. They found several mammoth teeth, jaw fragments and a few vertebrae. My guess is the site dates from probably 20,000 years before the present and represents the Columbian Mammoth, Mammuthus column.

The letter is signed by the collection manager of the Division of Vertebrate Paleontology and indicates that within the museum the site has been designated as Locality Wt-10 and the fossils are numbered 513-46.

I came home from the trip with good memories and a bag of bones. I didn't smuggle them out of Mexico. There is nothing rare about them. All are rib bones from an animal called a gomphothere, whose only living relative is the elephant. Between these two, on the family tree, are wooly mammoths, mastodons, and the Columbian mammoth.

I recently learned that Dr. Carranza is still at it but now works in a different part of Mexico. I am sorely tempted, but I remember the heat. And the vultures. When I asked myself how, at the age of sixty-five, I ended up digging for fossils in Mexico, I go back to a geology course I took during my freshman year at college. Doctor Stewart was an engaging professor; his invitation to examine the earth closely has stayed with me. To this day, every time I look at an outcropping of rock, I wonder if there are fossils hidden inside.

We never know the road down which our experience and education will take us. We just might find ourselves, fifty years later, searching for shade, with vultures circling, on a rutted road in Mexico.

cinnamon rolls

These rolls are associated with a singular event: when friends gathered at our house for breakfast after the Easter Vigil service at St. Paul Church in Harvard Square.

dough:

2 packages yeast, active dry or compressed
¼ cup warm water
(lukewarm for compressed yeast)
1¾ cups milk
¼ cup sugar
1½ cups (¾ lb.) soft butter
½ teaspoon salt
4 eggs, slightly beaten
8 cups unsifted all-purpose flour

1. Soften the yeast in the warm water. Scald the milk; add the sugar and ½ cup of the butter, stirring until the butter melts. Let cool to lukewarm. Stir in the yeast and the salt. Beat the milk mixture into the eggs to blend well. Place the flour in a large bowl; mix in the egg-and-milk mixture, stirring until the liquid is well blended into the flour and the mixture forms a ball. Knead the dough on a floured board for about 5 minutes, kneading in about ¼ cup more flour as necessary, until dough is smooth and elastic. Let the dough rest for 5 minutes.

2. Roll dough into a ¼-inch-thick rectangle, about 12 by 36 inches. Spread about ⅓ cup of the remaining butter over the center third of the dough; fold the right third over the buttered section and spread ⅓ cup of the remaining butter over that surface. Fold the left third over the buttered section. Give the folded dough a quarter turn, and roll it again into a rectangle about ½ inch thick. Spread the center third of the rectangle with the remaining ⅓ cup of butter; bring the ends of the rectangle to meet in the center, then fold in half, bringing the edges together. Place dough in a greased bowl, cover, and let rise in a warm place until almost doubled, about 1 hour. Punch dough down, wrap in plastic film, and chill for at least 3 hours or overnight. The dough must be well chilled in order to work with it. You can store it in the refrigerator for as long as three or four days.

rolls:

1 cup sugar

1 tablespoon cinnamon

½ cup melted butter

glaze:

1½ teaspoons warm water

1 cup sifted powdered sugar

1. Combine the sugar with the cinnamon. Divide the dough into 8 equal-sized pieces. Work with one at a time, returning the remaining dough to the refrigerator each time. Roll each piece of the dough out on a floured board to a rectangle about 9 by 12 inches. Brush about 1 tablespoon of the melted butter on the dough. Sprinkle about 2 tablespoons of the cinnamon-sugar mixture over the butter. Roll dough as for a jellyroll, starting with the 12-inch side; seal the edge. Cut the roll into eight 1½-inch pieces. Repeat with another section of dough. Place 16 slices cut side up in a greased 9 by 13-inch pan, spacing rolls ½ inch apart. You will need ¼ of the dough to fill the pan.

2. Let rise until rolls are nearly doubled in size, about 45 minutes. Bake in a moderately hot oven (375°) for 20 to 25 minutes or until well browned. Cool slightly and glaze each pan of rolls with a mixture of the warm water and powdered sugar.

Makes 5 dozen 2-inch rolls.

LETTERS SAVED BUT HARD TO READ

DARWIN

THE HOUGHTON *SHAHNAMEH*

COMMONWEALTH OF MASSACHUSETTS

MIDDLESEX, SS.   PROBATE COURT

I, PAUL J. CAVANAUGH, Register of Probate Court for said County of Middlesex, having, by law, custody of the seal and all the records, books, documents, and papers of or appertaining to said Court, hereby certify the paper   hereto annexed to be   a

true cop y   of a   paper   appertaining to said Court, and on file and of record in the office of said Court, to wit:

Decree nisi on a libel for divorce brought by
Mary M. Buffett of Cambridge, in said County
of Middlesex, against William N. Buffett of
said Cambridge.

I also certify that on November 10, 1973,
six months from the date of said decree nisi
having expired, and the Court not having
otherwise ordered, said decree of divorce
became absolute.

IN WITNESS WHEREOF, I have hereunto set my hand and affixed the seal of said Court, this ...second............................... day of
November............................... in the year of our Lord one thousand nine hundred and ....seventy-eight.........

PAUL J. CAVANAUGH............................... Register.

William F. Crishahy
Asst. Register

jmd

PING-PONG PARTNER

BEN, MY FRIEND

"MY HERO!"

AS VULTURES CIRCLED

WAGNER, *TRISTAN*, AND ME

PALM NUTS FOR CHRISTMAS

DEAR WILLA

Kent Krotter: In Memoriam

Kent Krotter, a classmate of mine at Carleton and a fellow Nebraskan, died six years ago. I wrote the following for our class newsletter.

Recently word came from the college that one of our classmates, Kent Krotter, had died in 2002. With it came the name and address of a sister, Alison Johnson, living in Maine. I had a special relationship with Kent. Though we were not close, Kent and I both came from Nebraska and his father was a big fan of one of my uncles, a conservative four-term Republican Congressman, Howard Buffett.

I wanted to tell Alison this and that I remembered Kent as a plain-spoken, good-hearted person of sound character. I knew nothing of his life from the time we graduated until his death in a nursing home in Indiana, but I wanted to tell her that if she ever came to Boston, I would enjoy meeting her for lunch. She called me three days later.

Over the phone she told me about a memoir she'd written about the Krotter family that she hoped one day to publish. She read me the first two paragraphs of Chapter One:

"Two tons of silver and gold coins, hundreds of thousands of nickels, dimes, quarters, and gold pieces. They were under our beds, in the kitchen cupboards, up in the attics, in the bottom of dresser drawers, in holes in the ground. My father was obsessed with gathering up these coins and hiding them away in any likely spot in the various houses and garages and store buildings he owned in our tiny town on the Midwestern prairie. Nothing could shake his belief that the total collapse of the American economy

and government was just around the corner, a collapse that would bring anarchy and rioting in the streets. With this shadow of Armageddon always hanging over him, Dad believed that he could save his family from disaster only by collecting as much gold and silver as he could lay his hands on.

"This fear of a future calamity that might leave his family penniless so dominated Dad's thoughts that he failed to see how his blind absorption in amassing wealth created family problems that would lead to his oldest son's hopeless alcoholism and his wife's mental collapse. My sister grew up so insecure that she eventually turned to the stars for answers to the frustrations of her life, immersing herself almost totally in the study of astrology. In the fairy tale, King Midas's daughter was miraculously restored to life after she had been turned to stone by her father's desire for gold, but Dad's destructive influence on his family could not be reversed."

Alison graduated summa cum laude from Carleton three years behind Kent. There is an article about her in the fall Voice [the Carleton alumni magazine] with a subheading: "Documentary filmmaker Alison Johnson '60 spreads the word about health problems among first responders, cleanup workers, and residents exposed to the dust and smoke from the World Trade Center attack."

She and I met for lunch in Cambridge. She brought along a copy of the 207-page family memoir. The table of contents includes brief comments about each chapter. As I scanned it, Kent's name stood out:

Mother learns Kent is drinking.

We bring Kent to Colorado for treatment by Mom's psychiatrist.

We learn that Kent is no longer working, is living with a manic-depressive woman, and is in the clutches of a confidence man.

Kent's house is foreclosed; he is found freezing to death in an alcoholic stupor in a house with no heat or running water; he attempts suicide; he ends up living in the Salvation Army.

The main themes of the book are the disposition of the coins—two tons of them—the mother's illness, and the father's disorientation following a severe heart attack. At the end of the memoir Alison includes the death certificates of both parents.

"Otherwise," she said, "no one would believe that they died on the same day in different states."

Given Kent's father's high regard for my uncle, it is only natural that he would seek out Howard's son, Warren Buffett. Alison sent Warren a copy of her manuscript. In 2006 she received a response:

DEAR ALISON,

In a sad way I enjoyed reading the account of your life and that of your father. It's a saga relating how an obsession with money can really mess up a family.

I only have vague memories of meeting your dad—it was a very long time ago. I do remember, however, the look in his eyes when he started talking about gold (and didn't stop!). I've seen it in other people and it's not a healthy signal. . .

We had another family connection. At some point, Mr. Krotter decided that the local schools were not good enough for his youngest child, Eric. Alison thinks it was in talking with Warren that Mr. Krotter learned of the school where I was teaching, New Trier Township High School, in Winnetka, Illinois. The man bought a house nearby, and Eric entered New Trier. Alison thought he'd been a student in one of my history classes and, on seeing a picture of him as a teenager, I remembered the boy.

On our way out of the restaurant, Alison said, "I think Kent was the nicest and kindest of us all."

In thinking about Kent Krotter's life I'm reminded of the great influence our families have on our lives. This is certainly true of Kent. I also recall the title of one of Willa Cather's novels—she is another Nebraskan—*One of Ours*. Kent Krotter, Carleton Class of 1955, will always be one of ours.

Wagner, *Tristan*, and Me

I had an epiphany recently at a Metropolitan Opera performance of Wagner's *Tristan und Isolde* in New York. I had bought my ticket online and taken the train down from Boston. I don't do this often, but I love Wagner. The performance had received raves, and I longed to bask again in the glorious music.

What made this performance so powerful? My answer is simple and too unsophisticated for the schooled operagoer or the music critic of the *New York Times*. No matter. I'll get to what happened soon. Yes, the voices were beautiful and up to the task—both Tristan and Isolde have demanding roles with long arias. My familiarity with the music helped. But what really mattered? For me, the evening felt like a homecoming. First, some details.

I'm not familiar with opera's current stars, but I knew the conductor, Daniel Barenboim, a world-famous musician who had never before appeared at the Metropolitan. Before the curtain rose on the final act a man stepped onstage to announce that the woman singing the role of Isolde, Linda Watson, was suffering from a cold and would be replaced by one Susan Wilson. There were no groans—always a good sign—and Ms. Wilson sang superbly. Leaving the performance, I heard one connoisseur say to another something about Ms. Watson's singing "off key several times towards the end of Act 1." Analysis at that level is beyond me.

My ear may be limited, but toward the end of Act II, when Tristan sings of his mother's death, something unexpected occurred; I felt something I'd never experienced before. Another opera by a different composer wouldn't have worked the same magic. Wagner's music and Tristan's words were essential, and something of my experience with Wagner and my parents is in order.

For a long time I had loved opera but avoided Wagner. His music sounded jarring and unfathomable, his stories ridiculous—full of impossible events and improbable consequences. A favorite *New Yorker* cartoon stayed in my memory. The full-page drawing showed the backstage of an opera house just before the curtain went up. The cast, sporting Wagnerian outfits, holding spears and shields, and wearing horned helmets, waited expectantly. A little man is running across the stage in front of the assembled cast. The caption: "My God, the orchestra is playing the overture to *Carmen.*"

But thirty-five years ago, a friend urged me to enter Wagner's world of myth and mystery, of gods and grandeur. We bought tickets for *Tristan und Isolde*, and several weeks before the performance, I bought the recording. I put the music on and thought "NEVER!" I listened again and thought, "Well, maybe." On the third try, I felt a resounding "Wow," and have responded that way ever since.

In *Aspects of Wagner,* author Bryan McGee claims that more has been written about Wagner than anyone except Jesus and Napoleon. McGee believes that operagoers either hate him, as does my wife, or love him, as I do. More than any other composer, Wagner seeps into the unconscious and stirs our deepest emotions.

On the night of January 11, 1974, my friend and I settled into our seats. Our only concern was that the performance actually happen. From gossip in the press we'd learned that the scheduled Isolde had canceled due to illness and been replaced. Then the scheduled Tristan backed out. The conductor, Erich Leinsdorf, expressed disapproval.

But as the starburst lights rose to the ceiling, the house lights dimmed, and applause greeted Leinsdorf's entrance into the pit, I relaxed. He raised his baton, and from the first notes of the overture I felt confident that this story of tortured love would faithfully unfold.

The next day, a front-page article in the *New York Times* announced "A Star Is Born," referring to Klara Barlow, the Brooklyn-born last-minute choice to sing Isolde.

In subsequent years I've heard many Wagner operas, some several times. During one performance, tears filled my eyes. I was at *Die Walküre,* the second of Wagner's four-opera Ring Cycle. Toward the end, Wotan, the chief god and father of Brünnhilde, decides that his disobedient daughter must be punished. He requires her to sleep on a rock surrounded by flames so high that none but the bravest of heroes can break through to claim her for his bride. The father and daughter are at the foot of a lonely rock where Wotan bids Brünnhilde a long and poignant farewell. Wagner's music conveys both the father's love and his sadness. I thought of my own daughter and for a brief moment became Wotan saying goodbye to my Wendy. Deep inside, I wept.

As I sat at the Met recently, another powerful moment took place. It came near the end of the second act of *Tristan und Isolde* when Tristan, recalling his mother, sings to Isolde:

> . . . it is the dark land of night
> from which my mother sent me forth
> when he whom in death she conceived
>
> in death she let go
> into the light
> there where she bore me
> which was the refuge for her love,
> the wondrous realm of night.

Confusing? It is for me, too. Listening to Wagner, I often don't get the meaning of all the words. What helps at the Met is the synchronized translation on a small screen in front of each audience member. But even the English isn't always comprehensible. That night, I didn't get every word but saw some go by in chunks: "my mother sent me forth . . . she let go . . . the refuge for her love . . . the wondrous realm."

Accompanied by the music, these words flooded me with a feeling from over seventy years ago: I felt my parents' love—not as I did in later life, but as I had as a baby and young child. Sitting in the darkened opera house, I didn't remember, imagine, or recall their love. I FELT IT.

What characterized my relationship with my parents in the intervening seventy-five years? I'd spent a lot of time thinking about those relationships and a lot of time in therapy. With its focus on my family of origin, therapy uncovered plenty to blame my parents for, especially my mother. At the age of three, I was left for several weeks on my grandmother's farm far away from home. When I recalled killing a kitten by bashing its head against a barn, the therapist thought the act expressed anger at being left without my parents. As a toddler, I had metal devices put around my thumbs to prevent my sucking them. I wet the bed for many years and, in grade school, had to wear knickers long after they went out of fashion.

My father worked twelve hours a day, six days a week. Though they had a wonderful marriage, my mother found my father reluctant to talk about feelings or to participate in cultural events. So she and I went together to various musical performances around the city. The therapist suggested that since my father was unavailable, my mother made me her companion—a tricky position for a young son. Going to a concert with Mom was different from going to a football game with Dad. A childhood photo of me with my mother makes me imagine her as a guard at a Nazi concentration camp where I am her prisoner.

But on the outside and in many ways my life and upbringing were fine, normal. I grew up in a stable middle-class home in Middle America. We went to church; my father owned a grocery store. And my mother's base was our home on Hickory Street, tending her two sons and having dinner on the table when we sat down around 6:30 P.M. I was a Boy Scout, sang in the church and high school choirs, had a girlfriend, and graduated from high school. I went to college and graduate school, then took a high school teaching job. I got married, had two children, and moved East for a doctoral program at Harvard.

Still, I'd long felt insecure in my identity and at times depressed. Certain things bothered me, and I could not resolve them on my own. When my marriage deteriorated and finally ended, I again sought out a therapist and saw that my life hadn't been a bust. I'd been president of the student government at my alma mater, was named a "master teacher" at the high school where I taught, earned a doctorate, and was the father of two fine children. My life began to improve.

After my parents died, I found an old letter I'd written to my brother and sister-in-law while I was living by myself in a cabin. Penned when my parents were visiting me, it said: "The other night Mother walked into the kitchen with tears in her eyes and said, 'I know you think we've ruined your life.'"

When I read those words now, "shame" isn't strong enough to describe my feeling. The letter identifies the nadir of our relationship. Thankfully, in time, it got much better.

Twenty years passed. I'd made my peace with my father, and I still cherish the words he spoke when I came from Boston and walked into his room at an Omaha hospital: "You're a sight for sore eyes." He died a few days later.

My mother and I had many more years—she died at the age of ninety-eight—to enjoy a lively and loving relationship. Helen Perea, a fine woman who cared for my mother in her final years, said something I will always cherish. One afternoon when I was visiting Omaha, Helen and her daughter Lola were at our family home. They would always retire to the kitchen while I talked with my bed-ridden mother. During a break, I walked into the kitchen where they were sitting. Helen looked up and said, "Lola and I were just saying that when we're as old as your mother, we hope we have a son like you."

But even at that time, I remembered a recent phone conversation with my buddy from kindergarten, Jim Olsen. In talking about our past, Jim said, "I know my parents loved me." I was struck by the fact that I couldn't bring myself to echo his words.

After she died, I wrote a book about my mother called *Dear Katherine*. In preparing it, I went though the daily diaries she kept for many years. Though not quite as often as she recorded her weight, she mentions my brother and me—speaking both of her devotion and worries.

Growing up, I didn't think much about my parents' love. I assumed all parents loved their children. Later in life, I knew they loved me, but we didn't talk much about such things. So, when sitting in the Met at seventy-five I experienced full-on the deep love they felt for me when I was a baby, I couldn't help feeling overwhelmed. I felt their protection, their caring, their hope, but above all, their deep and abiding love. In my bones and my blood, I felt it.

Again, Bryan McGee: "My central contention . . . is that Wagner's music expresses, as does no other art, repressed and highly charged contents of the psyche. . . . Some people are made to feel by it that they are in touch with the depths of their personalities for the very first time. The feeling is of wholeness yet unboundedness—hence, I suppose, its frequent comparison with mystical or religious experience."

Before hearing my most recent performance of *Tristan*, I'd always thought my life had three roots: Omaha, where I grew up; the farm where I spent every summer of my childhood; and Carleton College, where I thrived and earned a Bachelor of Arts degree.

That is what I'd thought. Now I know that behind those formative years, and more important than any other force, is the constant love of my parents. I recall the lines from William Faulkner's *Requiem for a Nun:* "The past is never dead. It is not even past." That night at the opera, Wagner's music proved the truth of those words.

edna kennedy's bird-in-the-nest

This is one of those dishes that both kids and adults enjoy. One of the greatest compliments I've received was when Maya, my granddaughter, told me my Bird-in-the-Nest was better than her mother's. I know why. I use more butter. Maya's mother cooks for health. I cook for grandchildren.

butter (for the pan)

1 slice **bread**

1 **egg**

begin with a small frying pan. Melt 2 to 4 tablespoons of butter. Take a slice of bread and make a hole in the center about the size of a ping-pong ball. Put the bread in the butter and turn it over quickly. Your aim is to get that side nicely coated.

break the egg so that the yolk falls into the center of the bread. Cook it slowly for about two minutes, then, being careful not to break the yolk, flip it over and cook for about a minute.

serve.

A Knock on the Door

I can't recall my favorite movie or book of 2009, but I have no trouble remembering my favorite knock on the door. It came from Alex Donis, age seven, who lives across the street.

"Want to come out and play?" he asked.

"Sure," I said, smiling. I am seventy-six years old.

The losses that come with age are well publicized—hair, hearing, sight, mobility, and memory—but I've lost something that isn't much talked about: my interest in self-help literature. I was once keen on having rock-hard abs, finding the "dream job," and learning Spanish in six weeks. Now I don't even pause when I see Donald Trump's new book *Think Like a Champion* or Michael O'Neill's *You Can Have What You Want* or an article that appeared in *Men's Health* thirty years too late: "Go All Night." (I even ignored a Viagra ad that popped up on my screen recently: "How to add more floors to your skyscraper.") And shame on *Prevention* magazine, once the champion of natural cures, organic foods, and a "back to nature" philosophy; emblazoned on the current issue's cover are the words NEVER LOOK OLD.

I am, however, becoming interested in information about getting older. I'm always looking for new perspectives and wise counsel. I found both recently in *Somewhere Near the End,* a memoir by Diana Athill, who is eighty-nine years old. She advises readers to keep young people in their lives as they age and describes the value of the young:

"[If] . . . flitting in and out of our awareness there are people who are beginning, to whom the years ahead are long and full of who knows what, it is a reminder that we are not just dots at the end of thin black lines projecting into nothingness, but are parts of the broad, many-colored river teeming with beginnings, ripenings, decayings . . . and our dying will be part of it just as these children's being young is."

At my age, invitations like Alex's don't come often. For half an hour, he and I, along with his father Joe and brother Andrew, played a sloppy game of street soccer. Andrew, age five, had as much trouble kicking the ball straight as I had moving fast. He lobbed a lot of balls into a driveway or flower bed, and when I tried to scramble toward an open ball, Joe invariably got there first. He gave no quarter. I tried not to. Alex and Joe were the stars, but everyone showed moments of passion. Lisa, Joe's wife and the boys' mother, came out to take pictures.

One of the reasons my wife and I remodeled our house, equipping it for our old age, is the presence of young families in the neighborhood. We keep a supply of toys in our front room cupboard—Legos, toy people, blocks, and an army of knights.

Sometimes when we're watching Alex and Andrew for their parents, and they get tired of toys and start tearing around the house, I remind myself that playtime will soon end, and the boys will return to the bosom of their family. I won't mind. As my wife's uncle says, "At Christmas time, the best lights are the tail lights."

Our friend Aimee and her daughter Amanda live next door to the Donis family. The other day Aimee had an early meeting at the homeless shelter where she works and asked if I could sit with Amanda from 7:45 until 8:00, when Lisa would take her to school. Raising a child really does take a village.

Just yesterday, as I got out of my car, Amanda asked if I could come and pitch. I did—first to Alex, then to Amanda, then to Andrew. I laughed a lot, mostly at my own ineptitude at catching the ball, throwing the ball, and retrieving the ball. I reminded myself that I'm no longer seventy-five.

I thumbed through *Somewhere Near the End* before buying it. I knew I could trust Athill when she said that, at eighty-nine, the main thing she misses is sex. And to her advice to have young people around she adds something that I hadn't realized: "One should never, never expect them [the young] to want one's company. . . . Enjoy whatever they are generous enough to offer, and leave it at that."

So thanks, Alex. Knock any time.

Palm Nuts for Christmas

Forgive the immodesty, but my creativity and sense of humor once bonded perfectly. It happened in December 2002. I prepared identical Christmas presents for five people, three of whom were my children. The gift—a small, round brown object nestled in a swath of cotton—was set in a gift box that was small, square, and white. A Christmas card and cover letter accompanied each little box. The letter began:

I'll tell you your present before you open the box. It's a palm nut. I found it lying on the ground—last August in Botswana. I brought several home, not knowing what I would do with them until, with Christmas approaching, I thought of you.

THIS PALM NUT:

Is NOT something you would ask for—EVER.
Is NOT something you've always wanted.
Is NOT something you've seen before.
Is NOT something you could buy in any store anywhere.
Is something only five people in the world will get for this
  or any other Christmas, birthday or Hanukkah.
Is NOT able, by fact or legend, to make you lucky, bring
  bad luck, or lengthen your life.
Is, though somewhat rare, not worth a dime and found only
  on one continent of the Southern Hemisphere.
You'll learn more about your palm nut when you open the box.
Like you, it has been through a lot, but "CAME OUT" okay.
It found light at the end of the tunnel.

AND SO WILL YOU.

This ended the cover letter. Recipients then opened the box and found the palm nut. They read the card that came with it:

PASS AS IN:

Sally PASSED *biology.*
Roger's car PASSED *the bus.*
Harry PASSED *the gravy.*
Ned PASSED *the ball.*
Congress PASSED *the law.*
Betty PASSED *Jane in the race.*
Dick PASSED *the message on to Tom.*
An elephant PASSED *this palm nut*

AND NOW IT IS YOURS.

The card also featured photographs of elephants and more commentary.

Elephants belong to the order Proboscidea. Long ago more than 160 species and subspecies of proboscideans roamed the planet. Today only two are left: the Asian and the African elephant. The African elephant is the world's largest land animal. Elephants and humans both live about seventy years and maintain the same lifelong family ties. [Elephants] can detect smells and hear sounds that we cannot. Elephant gestation takes nearly two years.

All elephants spend between ten and twelve hours a day eating and digest only about 44% of what they eat. They defecate about twelve times a day. (No wonder workers with brooms stay close behind circus elephants.)

I ended the card by answering some anticipated questions:

IS IT SAFE TO TOUCH THE PALM NUT? *Yes. Your nut spent months in the hot sun of Africa and endured freezing temperatures in New England. You are only the third mammal to come in contact with it.*

WHERE CAN I GET MORE OF THESE? *This nut will probably grow if you plant it. Then, all you need is an elephant—and patience.*

SHOULD I SAVE IT? *Yes. Your children will be asked to do a paper on elephants someday. Bringing this nut to class will amaze the teacher and guarantee a good grade. Holding the palm nut, with its unusual history, will be a first for any student brave enough to do so.*

I've always wished I'd come home with more palm nuts. One can never have too much of a good thing.

blueberry pancakes

This recipe has long been a favorite of family and friends. The secret is the nutmeg. Testers on a recent cooking show preferred milk and a tablespoon of lemon juice to the buttermilk. Without stating a preference, I'm sticking with buttermilk, mainly for old times' sake.

2 cups flour

2 tablespoons sugar

2 teaspoons baking powder

½ teaspoon each baking soda, salt, and freshly grated nutmeg (feel free to add up to a teaspoon of nutmeg)

1 pint blueberries, fresh or frozen

2 cups buttermilk

2 eggs

2 tablespoons vegetable oil

In a large bowl, mix the dry ingredients. Add the blueberries, then stir the liquid ingredients into the dry. Don't overmix. A few small lumps are fine.

Pancakes can be made any size that is flippable and can be cooked in a large frying pan; however, long ago I bought an electric griddle just for these pancakes. It works best. Grease the griddle lightly with an oiled paper towel. All the books say not to flip a pancake twice. I don't know what happens if you do. I've always gone by the books.

Dear Willa

DEAR AUNTIE WID,

This is my first letter to someone in Heaven, and I know you'll receive it. I'm now seventy-six and you died three years ago at the age of 95. You still mean as much to me as anyone including my mother, father, and brother. I miss you. You were the last person alive to see me the day I was born, and I've told many people that you were in my corner from that day on. How many can say they've had someone in their corner all their life? I was lucky.

You and I spoke rarely about the past. Wherever we were, whatever we were doing, our focus was on the here and now. Why this letter? To call it a trip down memory lane sounds thin and clichéd. Since we're no longer together here on earth, think of it as a brief review of our life together. Let me know where I need to fill in or if I make a mistake.

When I was seven, you were visiting our home in Omaha. One morning you and Mother were sitting in the front room. I came bounding down the steps, grabbed a decorative iron railing with one hand, a nearby desk lamp with the other, and froze. You got up, came over, and unplugged the lamp. That did it. I could move. It sounds too dramatic to speak of electrocution, but you sensed the current passing through me from a shorted-out lamp and rose to the occasion. Another time, on the farm, where I always slept on a bed of blankets next to Grammy's bed, I woke up one night howling. Fortunately, you were there. You got out of bed, found a flashlight, and looked in my ear. When a bug crawled out, its confusion ended along with my pain.

I always loved our time together time on the farm in South Central Nebraska, in part because it was where you, your twin brother William, and my mother Katherine were born. Not long ago I visited the site of District 9, your one-room schoolhouse near the farm. Corn grows where it once was, but your high school in Red Cloud still stands. Pictures of you and William hang there on a many-paneled wall of former graduates. While you and your brother received degrees from the University of Nebraska, my mother left early to make money so she could marry Fred Buffett, a grocer's son from Omaha. (Remember her story about how they met in a Spanish class, and as she used to say, "The only word I remember is *sí*"?) To this day I remain an enthusiastic fan of two teams, the Nebraska Cornhuskers and, more recently, the Boston Red Sox.

I'm not sure of your career right after the university, but I know you worked briefly at the YMCA in Omaha. By 1953 you'd moved back East and earned your doctorate in Vocational Education at George Washington University. For most of your career you were a professor at Michigan State. I regret that I never saw you teach a class.

As everyone knows, you remained single. My father and mother used to wonder if you died a virgin. He thought no, she thought yes. Fortunately you took the secret to your grave. If "old maid" lies at one end of the "single woman" spectrum, you were at the other. All of your life you remained attractive and modern—you traveled the world, became a life-long learner, sent $10 to every niece and nephew on birthdays, and enjoyed Chivas on the rocks.

To this day I'm amazed that unlike many raised on a farm, the three Norris siblings led lives far beyond Webster County. You, "Dr. Norris," published several books in your field. Your brother founded a computer company and was regarded as one of America's most innovative businessmen. My mother remained in a happy marriage for over fifty years, raised her sons, and was beloved by all who knew her. Your stories are unique, your lives filled with accomplishment.

The three of you returned to the farm for vacations. The place remained a taproot in your lives—as it has in mine. As a boy I went to the farm every summer. No land in all the world holds me in its spell as does Nebraska. My love for its land comes from the many days I spent on the farm helping John "fix fence," messing around in the tool shed, climbing up into the pasture, bringing in a basket of corn cobs for the wood stove, reading the Uncle Wiggly story in the daily *Nebraska State Journal,* eating Grammy's cooking, setting off fireworks in the front yard, catching fireflies in a jar, releasing the handle on the windmill so we could replenish the water supply, letting a newborn calf suck on my finger—life was full and adventurous.

One year, you were the University of Nebraska's May Queen. A picture of you in your May Queen gown hung just inside the front door. Part of the lore around your crowning involves finding a way for the family to pay for the gown. Your brother decided they'd kill a cow. Then there is the story of Grammy's sister-in-law, who lived down the road, calling to ask who May Green was. It was free entertainment back then to listen to each other's calls on the party line, and Mabel had heard "May Green" instead of "May Queen."

You and I weren't much for hugging and kissing. I was shy, and you seemed reluctant to risk a cold, but we were tight. Though plenty has been written about the relationship between parents and children, and surely grandparents are fondly recalled, not much out there explores the relationship between aunts and nephews.

When you arrived at the farm, Grammy and I were waiting. You and I often shared a Coke on hot summer afternoons, and you recalled our once being huddled together in the dining room when a rain, thunder, wind, and lightning storm was shaking the house. I asked if you were frightened. Reassured when you said no, I felt better, but years later you admitted you had been. When you visited I could count on your famous scrambled eggs: fry some chopped bacon, drain off the grease, then add beaten egg and chopped tomato.

And I remember your boyfriend, Chuck Peterson, and his visit to the farm. Chuck was large, balding, and robust. He laughed often. He didn't impress Grammy, though, when, trying to be helpful, he spilled the peach ice cream. She'd put fresh peaches, rich cream, and sugar in the metal canister that sat in a wooden bucket surrounded by salt and ice. Ice cream would eventually appear after someone turned a crank atop the canister.

It wasn't Chuck's lucky day. He was turning the crank on the steps between the back porch and the cellar house. One minute things were fine, but the next, the bucket and canister tipped over, and the soupy mix slopped slowly down the worn wooden steps.

Spilling the ice cream didn't win any points with Grammy, nor did Chuck's driving one Sunday afternoon when we were all heading for Red Cloud. Willa sat next to him. Grammy and I were in back. The road was a typical rural one: dusty and bumpy with plenty of curves and hills. To involve Grammy in the conversation, Chuck kept turning his head toward the back seat so she could hear, but I remember Grammy muttering, "If he doesn't watch the road, he'll get us all killed." Grammy, Chuck, her old Chevrolet, and even you have passed from the scene, but the road is still as it was.

I remember the train trip Grammy and I took in the summer of '42 to New York, where you were working on a master's at Columbia. Did I ever tell you that as we approached Penn Station I was talking to a solitary inebriated woman a few seats away? I was sweet-talking her into giving me some money, and was on the verge of success when Grammy called me back to my seat.

We stayed at the Taft Hotel, and I remember a joke the elevator man told me. "Mississippi, spell it." When I spelled Mississippi he chortled, "No, it's spelled I-T." I stopped by the place a few years back. Still a hotel, it has a new name. When I mentioned the Taft to a doorman, he told me that the only things they saved were the elevator doors. I walked in for a look, and there they were: big, bronze, and decorative. They don't make doors like that anymore, and there is no elevator operator to tell jokes to young boys.

You told me years later that we went to Coney Island but that you wouldn't go on a ride when I asked you to. We also ate at the Automat, where there were lots of little doors behind which sat various edibles. You put in the correct coins, opened the door, and took out a salad, a sandwich, a piece of pie, or anything else that looked good.

One incident scared me. Grammy and I were in our room at the Taft one night when all the lights, inside and out, went off. Sirens wailed, searchlights scanned the sky, and I fantasized Paul Bunyan, taller than any building, lumbering into Manhattan. In the morning we found out what had happened. Seven months into World War II, we were witnessing a practice air raid drill. Red Cloud seemed far away.

Our close relationship began at the farm and continued intermittently for many years, but the deepest experience we shared was going to the opera together. I don't remember how it started, but I got divorced about the time you retired from Michigan State, and over the years we met in New York many times.

Almost incomprehensible for me is that you and I met there in 1971 for an October 27 performance of Puccini's *La Bohème* and continued to meet in the Big Apple at least twice a year for thirty years. Occasionally we saw four operas in a weekend. I know because you made copies of each program's title sheet. Even in the worst winter weather we never missed a performance.

For example, on the night of Friday, September 17, 1976, we were settled in our seats in the Grand Tier, where you always liked to sit, for a performance by the Paris Opera of Gounod's *Faust*. I don't remember that performance but I'll never forget that the music got me out of my chair back in college. I must have told you the story. I was a freshman at Carleton, and one night, studying in my dorm, I heard some glorious music wafting down the hall. I followed it to Dick Keithan's room and knocked. Dick told me that the music was from the last act of *Faust*. I remembered Dick's recording and years later bought my own copy. It's an EMI recording with Victoria De los angeles singing the role of Marguerite, Nicolai Gedda in the role of Faust, and Boris Christoff as Mephistopheles. Though I've seen many performances of the opera, none has ever equaled that recording's final scene where Faust is urging Marguerite to escape with him from prison. She keeps singing "No" until Mephistopheles appears and pronounces her condemned. Then, as a chorus of angels pronounces her saved, the curtain slowly comes down as she ascends to heaven.

You and I have so many memories. We stayed at the Empire Hotel right across from Lincoln Center when it was a good second-rate hotel. We used to joke about its foibles, the occasional cockroach and the radiators that knocked in the night. We knew Ellen, a waitress at the attached restaurant, and Charlie, who lived at the hotel. Charlie talked fast, knew opera, and seemed to go through life like a fox—furtively and with beady eyes. Alice Wheelwright also lived at the Empire. She sat in a wheelchair, smoked, knew opera, and was a delight. I'd met her on a previous visit when I'd gone alone to New York, then introduced the two of you. For several years we would have dinner together at the Top of the Met, where Emil was our waiter.

Across Broadway, Fiorello's is still jammed before the opera and still serves that house salad you liked. Mary, the hostess—tall, middle-aged, attractive—has retired. We'd always hope she'd find us a booth. You'd start the evening with Chivas on the rocks with a little water on the side, while I stuck with Chivas and soda with a twist of lemon. Another ritual was my signing your credit card bill while you used the ladies' room. I did it so often, the forgery became easy.

Remember Monty, the short, heavy fellow who resembled Mr. Magoo and was outside the opera house before every performance, chatting and, I think, buying and selling a few tickets? He was mayor of the plaza in front of the house, a prelude to the opening curtain. My clearest memory of him was on the morning of December 31, 1972. I'd gone to New York for a New Year's Eve performance of Donizetti's *La Fille du Régiment* featuring Joan Sutherland and Luciano Pavarotti. The standing room line formed before 10 A.M., and I remember Monty working those assembled and muttering. When the curtain went up that night, I was behind the last row of the Family Circle, as far from the stage as possible, but remember a thrilling performance. I wish we could have heard it together, but I'm glad you didn't have to stand.

Among my life's most imaginative endeavors was the time I boarded the bus for New York in Greenfield and, along with a suitcase, brought a pot, a hot plate, and some asparagus. I'd mentioned to you that asparagus was ready in Franklin County and you regretted its being too early for the Michigan crop. I arrived, and several hours later we sat in your room at the Empire enjoying freshly steamed asparagus, one of your favorite vegetables.

You saved my many letters to you, most of them focusing on what we'd be seeing at the Metropolitan. Typically I'd listen to a recording, then suggest what to listen for:

Don Giovanni *has really grown on me this past week. (I keep thinking of a question once asked on Texaco's Opera Quiz. "Is there an opera that initially you didn't care for which you later came to enjoy?" One fellow's answer: "I listened to* Tristan und Isolde *five times and couldn't see what people were talking about, but then on the sixth time it finally came home to me.") Only in the past week have I been able to feel the lovely music in Mozart's opera.*

And later:

I think The Marriage of Figaro *is the one to study. It is hard to get straight. I've read Newman and also the chapter on* Figaro *in* Three Mozart Operas *by Robert Moberly. He does a thorough job of pointing out places where the orchestra—or even an instrument—echoes the action of the opera.*

You and I heard our first *Ring of the Niebelungs* by Richard Wagner in 1989, during the week of April 23–29. Hearing those four operas was a life experience. To prepare, we each got the new recording by Georg Solti on Decca Records. In a paperback, *Aspects of Wagner,* Brian McGee writes about this new recording, and I sent you some quotes:

"The Götterdämmerung *is regarded by many people as the best recording ever made of anything.* Gramophone *magazine called it "the greatest achievement in gramophone history yet," and* Records and Recording *said, "nothing like this* Götterdämmerung *has ever before come out of the recording studio."*

And I passed on what the critic Ernest Newman said about the entire work. "When criticism has said its worst about the *Ring* there remains nothing but to bend the knee and worship." I quoted from one of George Bernard Shaw's letters: "Even with totally incompetent performances of the *Ring,* we went around during the intermissions babbling with joy."

Your program for our *Götterdämmerung* is a reminder that we heard Hildegard Behrens as Brünnhilde with James Levine conducting, in a performance that began at 6 P.M. and ended at 11:40 P.M. You were tougher than I, and though you'd dole out a few mints before the curtain went up to stave off fatigue, I'd still feel your nudge if I nodded off.

You kept a written list of the operas you attended. It begins in 1961, when you heard a performance of *Madama Butterfly* in Rome. In subsequent years your record included operas in Munich, Verona, East Lansing, Detroit, Glyndeborne, and Salzburg. Then there is the *La Bohème* we saw at the Metropolitan in February 1972 with Richard Tucker as Rodolfo, and on five different occasions you visited us in Massachusetts for performances by the Opera Company of Boston. During one of them, I was driving for Checker Taxi and gave you a ride, but I forget the size of your tip.

Once in my life I commissioned a work of art, a gift for you. I'd become friends with Rick Mills, a fellow taxi driver and an artist, and I asked him to do a watercolor of Lincoln Center. When he'd finished, this note accompanied his work:

GREETINGS—

The Hotel Empire and Lincoln Center. A bit of both.

Do you know those days in New York in late November when the light is cool, gray-white, and thin? Winter coming, certainly, but still a hint of warm sun and fall.

A light-valued frame, a wisp really, and ordinary glass would, I think, be right for this delicately colored drawing.

Enjoy, Rick Mills

Some of my letters expressed my affection for you. Following the death onstage of Richard Tucker, one of the Met's leadings tenors, I wrote:

I think of his death with sadness. It isn't only that he sang opera or was one of my favorite singers, but that through his 60's, though some said he couldn't sing as well as he once did, he hung in there; he stayed with it. In some way he remained true to his best, sort of a "damn the torpedoes, full speed ahead." It makes me sad when a person like that bows out.

Then there is you—art courses, opera, travel, birds, photography, illustrated talks on angels, and on women of the Bible. You too are hanging in there and being true to who you are. As I am saddened by Tucker's death, I delight in your life. I want you to know that here in Massachusetts there is, not so much a nephew looking at an aunt, but Bill Buffett looking at Willa Norris and saying, "Amen."

Continuing courage to you—right on—and much love, Bill

And there's this from a letter I sent before one holiday: "I just wanted you to know that I am thinking of you and will miss your presence, charm, wit, good looks, trim figure, enthusiasm, and shining countenance this Thanksgiving."

In another letter I spoke of one of our favorites novels, Willa Cather's *My Antonia,* and recalled a scene where Jim speaks of being at the University of Nebraska and taking his girlfriend, Lena, to several plays. He says: "I like to watch a play with Lena; everything was wonderful to her and everything was true. It was like going to revival meetings with someone who was always being converted."

I added, "That's what it's like going to operas with my aunt."

Sometimes I veered away from the opera. I'm sure you remember this night. In a letter to my brother Fritz and his wife Pam, I wrote:

Thursday night we had dinner on the 107th floor of the World Trade Center at its restaurant, Windows on the World. As expected, the view is spectacular and the smell of money abounds. If I had to pick one word to sum up New York, it would be "class," real upper-crust class. The food was good and we got on so well with our waiter that he brought us an extra dessert, a sundae—sliced fresh mango and a gooey nut sauce over a big scoop of vanilla ice cream.

In one letter from when I drove a taxi, I told you about my children:

The children slept over at my apartment on Tuesday night. I pick them up at their mother's on Gurney Street, then we head for the supermarket. If I've metered between $30 and $40 we have $1.50 to spend, if it's between $40 and $50 we have $2.00, and if I meter over $50 it's $2.50 to spend. Tuesday we had $1.50 and with it we got a half a gallon of milk— 76 cents—a package of bean sprouts—53 cents—and a loaf of bread. We looked around for something that cost 21 cents. The closest we came was frozen green beans for 28 cents. Wendy wanted to go over budget but Tommy had the idea of saving the 21 cents and adding it to the amount for next week. So that's what we did. With some things I already had in the fridge, we had cold chicken wings left over from the night before, sautéed bean sprouts, and a green salad. All in all it was a pretty good meal.

While our relationship focused on opera and the farm, I twice initiated something silly. You spoke several times of an item then in the news: the spread north of killer bees. I parlayed that into a series of postcards from a fictitious Dr. Hanni Benin, head of the WFKB—the World Federation of Killer Bees. You were appointed head of the North America Quadrant of the WFKB, because you were among the few aware of the threat. The postcards showed gear to protect against their sting, pictures of people who'd been stung, and a photo of a Bavarian castle, which I identified as the WFKB's World Headquarters.

Another series followed my trip to Egypt, when I found a stamp depicting the head of King Tut. Beside the purple-colored Pharaoh, I'd have him speaking some rhyming witticism:

> You have a new car
> Don't dent a fender
> Here I am
> In all my splendor.
>
> Yours, TUT

I can't deny looking through these cards with some embarrassment, but I know I had fun sending them and guess you enjoyed finding them in your mail.

Yesterday I watched again the DVD my Norris cousins prepared on your life. "Amazing Grace" is sung in the background while photographs of your life come into view. My "Willa" file includes a photo of you as a member of the Red Cloud High School girls' basketball team. Toward the end of the disc is a photo of us taken a week before you died. The look on my face is one of love, while yours retains its determination and assurance. Susan took the picture, and she often quotes your last words to her: "Now you take good care of him. If you don't I'll reach down and squeeze your neck. And I won't be reaching up."

Your beauty shone through so many times. In a folder on Fritz, who died of kidney cancer shortly after his 60th birthday, I found a copy of your birthday card to him. You wrote:

You are one of my personal heroes—full of kindness, sensitivity, love and warmth. Oh yes, I rejoiced this day 60 years ago when you were born. Thank you for being, dear Fritz, just as you have been: thoughtful, gregarious, willing. You are an invaluable source of inspiration for courage, optimism and compassion. I love you Fritz and I always will.

This is the Red Cedar River and you may see a few ducks. Remember when your two little girls fed them long years ago? —Willa

Many times I've started a journal only to stop after a few days. I recently came across an entry dated August 5, 2006.

We buried a dear friend yesterday, my aunt of ninety-five years, Willa Norris. She'd been cremated in Minneapolis, and her ashes brought to Omaha by my cousins. We gathered at her grave site at the Forest Lawn Cemetery. Willa bought her plot many years before, and the headstone was in place. It now says simply, "Willa Norris 1911–2006." She rests next to my mother, Katherine Buffett, and my father, Fred Buffett.

It was a beautiful August day. There was a canopy to protect the mourners against the sun, which went unused. There were chairs. They too were unused. We stood in a circle around the hole. There were several bunches of flowers and a small table on which rested the urn containing Willa's ashes. Present were Nancy Brinks, the officiating pastor; Connie Van Hoven, a niece, and her husband, Greg; Mary Keck, a niece; Brian Norris, a nephew, and his wife Patty; David Norris, a nephew; Howard Norris, the son of William, another nephew; and me, with my wife, Susan Kennedy.

There was more to the service, but I didn't write it down.

Not long ago your nephew's daughter Danielle was married in San Francisco. After the reception dinner, pictures were taken. There's one of Mary, Connie, and me. Before the shutter snapped, Connie said, "Let's give the Willa salute." Remember? You'd make two fists and raise them shoulder high, then give a slight shake to both.

Thank you for being, dear Willa, just as you have been. I'll always be in your corner.

With much love, Bill

I Can Still Change a Light Bulb

Yes, I can still change a light bulb.

You're thinking, that's no big deal.

I agree, to a point.

We've all changed hundreds—bulbs in table lamps, kitchen lamps, ceiling fixtures, you name it. The only problem might be a dead bulb too hot to remove, a new bulb and empty socket that don't come together right away, or a lamp you forgot to plug into the wall socket. Simple problems, easy solutions. A minute later, light.

Change a light bulb? You think: no big deal.

I agree, to a point.

I've reached that point. Not long ago, a bulb from our dining room ceiling fixture died. Even with volts, watts, wires, and the power grid waiting, I knew the bulb wouldn't self-repair. I got the stepladder from our garage and a bulb from the box in the hall closet. I opened the stepladder, set it beside the table, and with a new bulb in hand, prepared to climb the two steps. At exactly that point, changing a bulb moved beyond the category "No big deal."

I turned seventy-six this year. I feel blessed to be healthy and alive but am no longer able to change this bulb without a touch of fear, hesitation, and a sense of wonder. Not wonder as in "awe," but wonder as in "Will I make it?" I took the job slowly, holding the bulb in one hand and, with the other, steadying myself on the edge of the table.

The fixture is hard to describe. Two bulbs sit inside an opaque dish that is held in place by a circle of steel. Three steel spokes connect the dish to the inner fixture and are secured by three little ball-shaped screws. I reached over and unscrewed one of the little balls. Unexpectedly, the dish slipped but didn't fall. My anxiety spiked, but nothing broke—including me.

The dead bulb, on the far side, came out easily. Replacing it proved more difficult. Unable to see both the end of the bulb and the empty socket made matching their threads difficult. I fumbled around, but after several tries, voila! Tricky, too, was screwing the little ball back on. I needed one hand to steady the dish, the other to replace the ball. My left arm grew tired. Would the ball behave? Would I find its little hole? Could I get the threads to match?

I managed.

But where was my old confidence? I never imagined that someday I'd feel shaky changing a light bulb. The experience became a turning point on my road to getting older. Eventually, the task will become too difficult. Someone else will have to attend to it. I've got my eye on Alex, age seven, who lives across the street. I hope he becomes my bulb boy when we're both older.

If it's natural to think more often about aging when one is in his seventies, then I'm a natural. Aging is on my mind as I walk, more slowly; as I see, not as well; and as I hear, most of the time. This awareness isn't constant, but reminders pop up.

Several months ago I was having breakfast alone one morning in a hotel in California. An older couple sat down at a table behind me. I caught a glimpse of the African-American waitress approaching and heard the man say, "How about a cuddle?" Ah, I imagined, he's a familiar customer or a good friend. But the fantasy crashed when the waitress asked for clarification.

"An avocado?"

"Yes," he replied, "sliced."

I laughed. But I didn't the other morning when I rose at 5:30 and ambled to the dresser. Just as I opened my sock drawer—Pow! A spasm, crick, or pinched nerve stabbed at my lower back. I barely made it back to bed, where I sat until able to hobble to breakfast. This was new.

I've never forgotten the words of an old gent I drove home from the hospital back in my cabbie days: "Yes," he told me, "as long as you can get up in the morning and put your own clothes on you have an awful lot going for you."

Eventually, I put on my own clothes that morning. I may have a bulb boy lined up, but not a valet.

Just as I've never heard anyone say they like to move, look for work, or go to the dentist, I've never heard anyone say they like getting older. But there are advantages. What? Yes, this is contradictory—aware of the benefits after saying there aren't any? But my defense can be found in lines from Walt Whitman's *Song of Myself*:

> Do I contradict myself?
> Very well then, I contradict myself.
> (I am large, I contain multitudes.)

Like every older person, I now contain more multitudes.

Recently, I met a friend for lunch who I don't see often. As we sat down he said, "Bill, older is better." (I'm contradicting myself again. Nobody is supposed to say they like getting older.) For those who aren't "older," the idea that older is better must be hard to believe. But listen to this— one of my favorite passages from Chekhov's short story "In the Ravine." (The setting is a rural area on a sunny day. Several characters wait for an old woman to catch up. We feel their impatience.)

Then along came Praskovya, gasping for breath. Her wrinkled perpetually anxious face beamed with happiness. That same day she had gone to church, then went along to the fair and had a drink of pear kvass. This was so unusual for her that now she felt for the first time in her life, she was really enjoying herself.

What is so good about being older? Praskovya would have her own answer. I have mine. At the top of my list is that after earning two master's degrees and a doctorate, and having taught high school history for eleven years, I no longer have to write papers or take tests. That I don't have to study or learn a foreign language or go to work every day are other reasons I'm glad to be older.

I do not say "old." Regardless of how others define the term, I can't yet think of myself as old. I have no problem with "getting older." I see evidence when I look in a mirror, get out of a chair, or stagger to the bathroom in the middle of the night. And I hurled a foul epithet at *Time* magazine recently when it defined anyone over sixty-five as "elderly."

I shudder at being considered elderly. I wouldn't mind being thought of as an elder, a word that recognizes and welcomes my experience and assumes I have deep wisdom to offer. In my ideal world, people my age would be considered elders until they reach ninety; then— forced retirement. I wouldn't mind. Nothing lasts forever.

Leaving a health club the other day, I passed a man my age slumped and waiting at a table. A studly trainer with rippling abs approached: "Well, Frank, ready to kick some butt today?"

I added that to my list: I no longer have to kick butt, something I was never good at anyway.

These days, I'm pretty much free of stress or the need to hurry. I've been single and remember the hunt. I've been divorced and remember the pain. I've failed and remember the anguish; I've worked and remember the tensions. I have a roof over my head, food to eat, a good wife, and a fine family. The "wants" I have are mostly for other people—from people in my neighborhood who are having a tough time to people in the Congo suffering the ravages of civil war. I recently defined an ideal retirement as waking up in the morning with five things to do, none of which has to be done today. I'm having that kind of retirement. Yes, I know it could all end in a snap. I'm speaking only about today, the only thing any of us has anyway.

That I've reached my mid-seventies and feel this way is largely a matter of luck. I entered Carleton College in the fall of 1951, along with 257 other hopeful young men and women. In 2009, 56 were dead. That I'm not yet among them isn't a matter of wisdom or ethics. It is a matter of luck, with perhaps some good self-care thrown in. (I give myself a grade of B minus in eating right and getting exercise.)

Every day I check the obituaries. I'm interested only in those who merit an article and about these, only their ages. In today's *Boston Globe,* there were more than usual— three on one page, five on another. In section B, page 9, I read that Altovise died at 65, Ron at 62, Michael at 67. On page B10, I saw that Ian passed on at 82, Luther at 84, Boyd at 88, Peter at 89, and Joan, also at 89. Both pages give me a good feeling. One page says that there is still time ahead. The other page reaffirms my good luck.

A cousin of mine refers to what he calls "the ovarian lottery." Imagine, he suggests, there is this barrel containing a thousand pieces of paper. On each is written the name of a different continent, race, and class in society—all distributed in proportion to their actual presence on earth. For example, eight percent of the world's population lives in Africa. On eighty pieces of paper, the word "Africa" would appear. Those eighty would be further defined by the percentage that is black and poor and lives in the continent's various countries.

In this parlor game you have a chance to change places with someone identified on one of the pieces of paper. Would you do it? Probably not. This means you've won the ovarian lottery. Many factors that contribute to who I am are beyond my control. I'm a white male born in the early 1930s into an intact middle-class family in a stable neighborhood. I profited from good public schools. All were positive influences given gratis, by chance.

You sense, getting older, that you are no longer part of the preferred demographic and sometimes feel left out. Headlines on a recent cover of *Men's Health* blared, "Six Pack Abs!" and "How to keep yourself in shape at any age: 30s, 40s, 50s." Neither is aimed at my generation. Just when you really need help they write you off. The "Golden Oldies" section of a local record store went all the way back to the . . . 1960s! Where are you "Dear Hearts and Gentle People," "Buttons and Bows," and "Some Enchanted Evening"?

Even the daily horoscope is exclusive—of me. I'm an Aquarius, and yesterday my fortune read: "Consider retraining, additional education or starting your own business." "Fat chance," I muttered.

An expression that was funny at first but has grown tired and trite is "senior moment." I want to redefine the term. Not long ago I got up early, went quietly downstairs, put on the coffee, got the morning papers from the sidewalk, and settled down to breakfast. Amidst the dark and the silence, it occurred to me that I was having a senior moment, one I couldn't have had when children were around or I had to get ready for work. My definition speaks not of a deficit, but of abundance.

Last fall a friend of mine and I were sitting in the end zone at Memorial Stadium in Lincoln, Nebraska. Both of us are ardent Huskers fans. An aisle separated us from many rows of young, energetic students. He and I smiled about how happy we were that we didn't have to party after the game.

Though I have no wise words about growing old, several thoughts give me cheer or are cause for amazement. I like what the actress Helen Hayes once said: "The years from 10 to 70 are the hardest." And as Katherine Hepburn remarked: "I never lose sight of the fact that just being is fun."

An abiding source of amazement is this: Earth is part of our solar system, which is part of the Milky Way Galaxy. This galaxy of ours includes over 400 billion other stars and planets. Our galaxy alone is 100,000 light years in diameter, and light travels at the rate of 186,000 miles per second. There are billions of galaxies in the universe.

Consider us from another perspective. Our earth is about 4.5 billion years old. Humans appeared about 200,000 years ago. Considering the vastness of the universe and the years human beings have been around, to paraphrase Rilke, it is breathtaking simply to be here.

I gained a new role model the other day, a fellow I'd never heard of before named George Hanson. An article in the February 26, 2009, edition of the *Boston Globe* began this way. "Ninety-one-year-old George Hanson climbed a 7-foot ladder yesterday at M. Steinert & Sons piano store to change some fluorescent light bulbs. His boss, store manager Bob Bates, was alarmed. 'I had to actually threaten to fire him to get him down,' chuckled Bates."

Growing older? Keep in mind the old Spanish proverb: "Traveler, there is no way; the way is made by going."

That we're here at all is simply breathtaking.

granola from the harvey house

I make no claim that this is the best granola ever, or the one with the least fat, but since I asked for the recipe from the woman who owns the Harvey House, a bed and breakfast in Oak Park, Illinois, I've never been without it. I always make a double batch and hide it when company comes. I substitute chopped walnuts for the cashews.

3 cups rolled oats, 1 cup cashews, 1 cup slivered almonds, ¾ cup shredded sweet coconut, ¼ cup plus 2 tablespoons dark brown sugar

¼ cup plus 2 tablespoons maple syrup, ¼ cup vegetable oil, ¾ teaspoon salt, 1 cup dried cranberries

Preheat oven to 250° F.

1. In a large bowl combine oats, nuts, coconut, and brown sugar.

2. In another bowl combine syrup, oil, and salt.

3. Add the syrup to the dry ingredients and pour the mixture onto two sheet pans. Cook for 1 hour and 15 minutes, stirring every 15 minutes to achieve an even color and to break up lumps. Remove from oven and transfer to a large bowl. Add cranberries and mix.

open house recipes

In the past Susan and I hosted an annual Christmas open house. Someone said, "Bill, not only do I know what you'll serve, I know where everything will be placed." I think having a set menu and a place to put everything was the only way we managed. It never varied, but there were no complaints.

Ralph Hergert told me that around July 1 he began looking forward to my eggnog. Others referred to the event as our cookie party because, at its height, I made more than eighteen different kinds. I'd begin them weeks ahead of time, wrap the dough in plastic wrap, and then bake them a day or two before the big event. They were put in tins and taken downstairs to the workbench, a place I dubbed "cookie central." Just before the party began I'd place an array of them on my grandmother's large silver platter and take them upstairs.

I'm including three recipes: one for lemon bars, which were probably the odds-on favorite, Phyllis Noble's chocolate cookie recipe—Phyllis was the legal officer for many years at the Massachusetts Mental Health Center, where I worked—and the recipe for eggnog from the old *New York Times Cookbook.*

lemon bars

1½ cups flour

3 tablespoons sugar

¼ teaspoon salt

¼ lb. (one stick) cold butter or margarine

3 eggs

1½ cups dark brown sugar

¾ cup chopped pecans

¾ cup coconut

½ tablespoon vanilla

2¾ cups confectioner's sugar

Zest of 2 lemons

4 tablespoons lemon juice

1. Preheat oven to 350°.

2. In a medium bowl, mix the flour, sugar and salt. Cut in the butter until the mixture resembles coarse meal. Press into a 12 by 18-inch baking pan and bake for 15 minutes.

3. Mix the eggs with the brown sugar, pecans, coconut, and vanilla and pour over the partly baked pastry. Bake 20 to 30 minutes longer, or until topping is firm.

4. Mix the confectioner's sugar, zest, and juice until smooth, and spread over the second layer. Allow to cool.

5. Cut into 1 by 1½-inch squares. The bars may be frozen.

phyllis noble's chocolate cookies

1¾ cups flour

1 teaspoon baking soda

¾ teaspoon salt

6 oz. sweet cooking chocolate, cut up

4 oz. unsweetened chocolate, cut up

1 cup sugar

1 cup light brown sugar

2 sticks unsalted butter, cut into 16 pieces

2 large eggs

1 tablespoon vanilla

powdered sugar

1. Preheat oven to 375°.

2. Process in food processor flour, soda and salt for 5 seconds. Set aside.

3. Put ½ of each type of chocolate into the processor with ¼ cup of white sugar. Pulse 4 times to chop, then process for 1 minute until chocolate is as fine as sugar. Add ¼ cup white sugar and ½ cup brown sugar. Process for 30 seconds. Add ½ of the butter, ½ tablespoon of vanilla, and 1 egg. Process for 1 minute, stopping once to scrape the sides of the bowl. Add ½ of the flour mixture and pulse 5 times until flour disappears. Don't overprocess. Set aside. Repeat the process with the remaining ingredients.

4. Chill dough for about an hour then form dough into small balls and place 2 inches apart on an ungreased baking sheet.

chewy: Bake 8 minutes
crisp: Bake 9 minutes.

Cool 2 minutes. Remove and dust with powdered sugar.

eggnog

So highly do I think of this eggnog that I fantasize about having it be my last sip before expiring. (Mourners beware.)

12 **eggs**, separated
1 cup **sugar**
1 cup **bourbon**
1 cup **cognac**
½ teaspoon **salt**
3 pints **heavy cream**
Grated **nutmeg**

1. In an electric mixer, beat egg yolks and sugar at high speed until thick and lemon-colored. Slowly add bourbon and cognac while beating at slow speed. Chill for several hours.

2. Add the salt to the reserved egg whites and beat whites until almost stiff. Whip the cream until stiff. Fold the whipped cream into the yolk mix, then fold in the beaten egg whites.

3. Serve in punch cups with a spoon and grating of nutmeg on top.

This recipe makes about 40 cups.